T0294370

Two
Thousand
Games

BRIAN
HORTON

A Life in Football

Two
Thousand
Games

BRIAN HORTON

A Life in Football

with Tim Rich

First published by Pitch Publishing, 2020

Pitch Publishing
A2 Yeoman Gate
Yeoman Way
Worthing
Sussex
BN13 3QZ
www.pitchpublishing.co.uk
info@pitchpublishing.co.uk

A CIP catalogue record is available for this book
from the British Library.

ISBN 978 1 78531 668 5

Typesetting and origination by Pitch Publishing
Printed and bound in India by Replika Press Pvt. Ltd.

Contents

This book is dedicated to my wife, Val, and my children, Matthew and Lucy. To their partners, Emily and Simon. To Lucy's stepdaughter, Imogen. To Val's son Simon and grandchild Layla. It is also dedicated to all the players and staff I have worked with throughout my career.

Foreword by David Pleat

HAVING been fortunate to spend a wonderfully enjoyable career as player, manager and director of football, I have met many hundreds of characters in the game; the great, the not so great, the talents, the wasters, the good, the bad and the ugly.

I was honoured and proud to be asked to pen a foreword for this diamond of a man. He was and is without doubt the most influential person I have had the pleasure to be associated with in the game.

As a player, he was a rock, a captain courageous, an inspirational leader but, most of all, a trusted confidant on team matters while at Luton Town. He was a born leader, destined to be successful.

Somehow, I persuaded a man who had been revered at Brighton to head the 'project' on the field at Kenilworth Road.

I signed Brian after Peter Taylor, a lifelong friend, had assured me that: 'He will never let you down.' My assistant at the time, Ken Gutteridge, was equally adamant.

Bringing him to Kenilworth Road at the age of 32 proved to be a masterstroke as my young, exciting team of the early 1980s respected and trusted him as captain of a side that became everyone's second-favourite team.

In 1981/82, as we stormed the heights to become champions of Division Two, all in football recognised the contribution of my piratical figure, leading our imaginative team. He was the catalyst that catapulted Luton to the top flight.

Within the club, Brian was the glue. Players confided in him and trusted him as he ran the dressing room in his diplomatic style. The players would have sensed that he had my ear, too. He knew what to say and when to say it. They confided in him to such an extent because they knew he would never betray a confidence from either myself or from the playing staff.

He was a leader in every sense of the word, a man with committed principles, determined in all he did and possessed with a great will to win. At 32, he provided the example to help players at our cramped ground at Kenilworth Road become full internationals. Ricky Hill, Brian Stein and Paul Walsh were call capped for England while Mal Donaghy became a mainstay of the Northern Ireland team for many years.

Everybody reminds me of the way I danced on to the pitch at Maine Road after we had saved ourselves from relegation by beating Manchester City in 1983. They seldom mention that the first man I embraced on the pitch was Brian Horton.

His performances had so often made a difference to our club. We had relegated Manchester City but as I told their distraught chairman, Peter Swales, immediately afterwards if they went down, Manchester City would go back up because of the sheer size of the club. If little Luton Town were relegated, I feared we would never return to the big time.

As a wing-half, used centrally, he could tackle, pass precisely and was superb at providing cover when it came to clearing up danger. A fierce competitor, he ran a fine disciplinary line – more than once a referee looked petrified when encountering the 'Horton stare' after he had been punished for a midfield challenge. He almost seemed to make the referee feel guilty!

It was a nailed-on certainty that he would go on to manage over 1,000 games, to become a member of an exclusive group. All his qualities as a true leader came to fruition in management. When Don Robinson, chairman of Hull City, asked me for a view on Brian's suitability to lead his club, I told him with 100 per cent confidence that he could 'sleep easy at night' if he took him.

His subsequent career was exceptional. Dedicating himself to the 'impossible job' of football management, he survived falling off the managers' roundabout with graft, knowledge and people skills, mainly without the resources of grander clubs.

Experiencing the highs and lows, taking the twin impostors in his stride, he worked diligently from Hull to the biggest stage at Manchester City.

A tiny fraction of players begin at the bottom, in non-league football, and rise to the top. To go on and achieve the magic 1,000 games as a manager shows a wonderful dedication.

Brian Horton was special. A leader of men, a true gentleman and an example to any aspiring young footballer. I hope the book will be a great read.

David Pleat, March 2020

Sold for a Pint of Shandy

I WAS a miner's son born in a coalfield that is now largely forgotten.

The North Staffordshire Coalfield was not vast like South Wales or Yorkshire but tight, compact and full of pits. Before the First World War, Cannock Chase produced five million tons of coal a year. Hednesford, where I grew up, was a mining town. Its football team were known as 'The Pitmen'.

My father, Richard, whom everyone called Dick Horton, was a miner, who had a passion for horses – there was not a day that went by that he did not put a bet on one. His other passion was football and in particular Wolverhampton Wanderers.

When I was growing up, he would take me everywhere across the Midlands to watch a game but Molineux was special. We would sit on the wall behind the goal. Ron Flowers, who was my hero, Peter Broadbent and Norman Deeley were wonderful footballers.

When I first started watching them, Wolves were the best team in England. In 1959, when I was ten, they retained the league title. The next year, they won the FA Cup.

I was far too young to have gone but in 1954 they had beaten the fantastic Hungarian side, Honved, led by Ferenc Puskas under the floodlights of Molineux. It was the first time a white ball had been used in England and it made Wolves fans believe that they supported not just the best team in England but maybe the world.

If I wanted a pair of new boots, or the new white ball, my father would do a double shift at the pit. We lived on a Coal Board estate and in front of the houses there was a big field where we played. We made a football pitch on it and after a week all the white would have come off the ball.

My mum, Irene, worked as a cook at Cannock Grammar School. She was the one who ran our household. She was a very strong woman and it was perhaps from her that I got my character and determination.

My older brother, John, I don't think ever kicked a ball in his life. His passion was cars and he went on to own his own garage and became a very successful businessman.

My younger brother, Alan, was more academic than either of us and worked for the Professional Footballers' Association sorting out mortgages for players.

My father was not from a long-standing mining family. His father had a business building sheds and it was taken over by my uncle – Dick's brother. When my dad was injured in the mines, my uncle asked him to work with them and I watched them demolish an RAF camp in Wiltshire and then take away the biggest pieces of wood to turn into sheds.

However, they say that once you are a miner, you are always a miner. Dad couldn't stand a working life away from the coalface and he went back down the pit. He loved pit life, the miners' talk. Most nights he would put on his collar and tie and go down the pub to continue the conversations.

He died in a tragic accident. John owned the King Ford franchise in Stoke and sponsored many of the Stoke City players as well as Mark Lawrenson when he was at Liverpool.

John lived in a large house in Staffordshire and, after he had retired, Dad would come and work in the garden or help him with odd jobs around the house.

The house had a sweeping staircase that curved upwards. Dad wanted to climb up a ladder to clean a window but John's wife was about to go out and she said: 'Don't go up without me holding the ladder. It's not safe.' When she came back, she found my father dead at the foot of the stairs. He had gone up the ladder and fallen.

Much as my father loved mining and miners, he did not want any of his sons to follow him down the colliery shaft. When I was 15, I was taken down the pit. I was by then desperate to make it as a professional footballer but this was a reminder of where, if it didn't happen, I would be going.

Sport had been part of my life ever since I could remember. I was captain of the football team at my primary school, St Chads, where we won the league and cup and went to a secondary school, called Central, where sport was at the centre of the curriculum. We had two teachers, called Mr Hubbard and Mr Salter, who organised not just football and cricket but badminton and trampolining.

In January 1963 we were all moved to a new school, The Blake, which had been built on land once owned by the West Cannock Colliery Company and had been used to stockpile coal.

By then, I was playing for Staffordshire and then for Birmingham District and had met a teacher called Ron Bullas who became one of the most influential people in my life.

He was a schoolteacher who scouted for Birmingham City and ran a club called Cannock Athletic in the Walsall League. I played in their under-18 team when I was 11. Ron was way ahead of his time. He would take me and three or four others to the gym simply to practise skills, like keepie-uppies and drag-backs – the sort of thing that nobody else seemed to be doing at our level.

Because of Ron's connections to Birmingham City, we would go to the club's training ground at Elmdon, near the airport. I was driven down by Malcolm Beard, who was from Cannock and a regular part of Birmingham's midfield.

Birmingham were then a very powerful side, perhaps as good as they have ever been. Malcolm played for Birmingham against Roma in the 1961 Fairs Cup Final and was part of the side that beat Aston Villa to win the League Cup two years later.

The Midlands in the late 1950s and early 1960s was a hotbed of football. Wolves were the dominant team but Aston Villa had won the FA Cup in 1957 and the League Cup in 1961.

Birmingham didn't take me on as an apprentice but Walsall did. They were in the Third Division. I was 15, three years younger than Allan Clarke, who was already the star of Fellows Park. Like me, he had sat behind the goal at Molineux. He had been brought up a West Bromwich Albion fan but, from his home, it was one bus ride to Molineux and three to The Hawthorns.

Arthur Cox was a coach at Walsall and after training he used to keep the first-team goalkeepers back and allow Clarke to practise his finishing against him. He was one of those footballers that you knew would make it. In 1966, when he was 19, he was sold to Fulham for £37,500, which was then a huge sum of money for a teenager.

Ken Hodgkinson was one of the big personalities at Walsall when I was breaking into the reserves. He was just coming to the end of his career, an elder statesman of the dressing room.

Of the apprentices at Walsall, only me and a lad called Geoff Morris, who would become the youngest player in the club's history when he made his first-team debut, had really broken into the reserves.

We spent the summer of 1966, the World Cup summer, doing pre-season training and then the manager, Ray Shaw, offered me a lift to the bus station, which seemed very strange. As we were driving into town he said: 'We've made a decision not to keep you on for the third year of your apprenticeship.'

I could not understand what he was saying. I thought I had done enough. Ken Hodgkinson was gobsmacked I had been given a free transfer. I was broken-hearted. I was 17 and it was the end of my life. I had been rejected by Birmingham and now Walsall. I could not imagine where I would go from here. I wasn't just thinking of football. I had no profession.

There was a guy, Bryan Yates, who was married to my cousin, Jeanette Horton, who had a bricklaying gang. He played in goal for Hednesford Town and he knew where work could be found on the sites.

At the same time, I was asked if I wanted to play for Hednesford. I was working on building sites in Walsall and playing non-league football. Looking back, it was probably the best four years of my life.

The building work brought in decent money and my mum sorted out the tax. There would be match fees and win bonuses from Hednesford – and we won a lot. I was driving a Ford Anglia which had belonged to my brother.

I was then more of a forward than the midfielder I became. Their player-manager was Dick Neal, who had played for Lincoln and for Birmingham in the 1960 Fairs Cup Final against Barcelona.

He was sacked not long after I joined. His replacement was Granville Palin, whose great claim to fame was that he had been part of the Wolves side that had won the 1958 FA Youth Cup Final after losing the first leg 5-1 at Chelsea. They had scored six at Molineux.

I treated playing for Hednesford as if it were a full-time job. My mates would be taking the usual Friday night release down the pub and I would be with them with a Coca-Cola or an orange juice.

I grew up in a tight community and I still keep in touch with my school mates – 'Wink' Bakewell, John Blackham, Alan Dangerfield, Gary Willis and Micky Elcock – more than 50 years on. Gary and Micky were very good footballers and played alongside me at junior and senior school.

We would train twice a week, on a Tuesday and a Thursday and because the lights at our ground, Cross Keys, were sometimes not good enough for much ball work, we would go on road runs. I forged great friendships at Hednesford, particularly with Billy Millard, to whom I was best man at his wedding.

Hednesford had former pros like Jimmy Campbell and Ray Wiggin, who had played for West Bromwich Albion and Walsall, and they were not playing for the sheer love of the game. They wanted the win bonuses.

I had known from an early age how much these mattered. When I was a teenaged apprentice for Walsall, I was playing for the reserves at Dudley Town and I cost them a goal. I was the last man in the wall but they were clever, played the free-kick past me, and a lad ran across and scored.

My team-mates went absolutely berserk. They slaughtered me because I had cost them the game and cost them their win bonus. Ken Hodgkinson, who was Walsall's senior pro, went over to me and said: 'You'll never do that again, will you?' I never did.

My gaffer on the building sites around Walsall was a workaholic called Harry Bann. We would build the inside walls once a house had its roof on and Harry's schedule was to do a house a day. Once I had done a wall, usually with breeze blocks, Harry would come over, check it and then it was on to the next one.

I loved building sites and their conversations. There would be Irish plasterers who always had a story. There would be others who were football daft. We would stop for a sandwich and some football talk. Combined with training two nights a week with Hednesford, it made me astonishingly fit, strong and tough.

We worked the same site in Walsall for several years and then went over to a new job at Sutton Coldfield. When I arrived, Harry was not there which was very unusual. I carried on with the work and went in the next day.

That morning there were police on the site. They said: 'We've come about Harry Bann. He's committed suicide.' They had found him in his car, dead. I was devastated. I had worked next to him for four years.

He was one of the happiest men you could wish to meet. However, his wife had had a baby, she suffered from post-natal depression and he had met someone else. Everything fell apart and he ended his life with an overdose in Sutton Park.

I was on my own but I had learned enough to carry on doing walls by myself. However, at Hednesford things were changing.

In 1970 we beat Kidderminster Harriers to win the Staffordshire Senior Cup, which turned out to be my last game for Hednesford. Gordon Lee, who was the manager of Port Vale, had been watching me and was now ready to make an offer.

Before joining Aston Villa, Gordon had played for Hednesford and continued to follow the club. Port Vale had just won promotion to the Third Division but they had no money, there was no question of a transfer fee but he told the club secretary that he would buy him a pint of shandy from the club bar, 'to make it worth your while'. The story Gordon told was that I had been sold for a pint of shandy.

I was, in fact, sold for more than a mixture of lager and lemonade because Port Vale agreed to play a pre-season friendly in which Hednesford would keep all the gate receipts.

At Hednesford one of the supporters had told me I played like Nobby Stiles. When I returned with Port Vale to play the friendly at Hednesford, the players heard me being called 'Nobby' and the name has stuck with me forever. It was not a bad player to be named after.

Although it was what I had wanted since I was a boy it was not an easy decision to become a professional footballer. I was 21 when Gordon Lee approached me and I had more or less abandoned the idea of being a pro. I thought those dreams had passed.

At Walsall I had earned £6 a week as an apprentice. I was now a self-employed builder who could reckon on about £20 a week. Hednesford paid £7 a week but with bonuses that would come to another £20. All in all, I was earning about £40 a week. In today's money, that was £600. I was still living at home so I had plenty of cash. The Anglia had been upgraded to a new Ford Cortina GT.

Port Vale offered me £23 a week. To become a professional footballer would mean taking a pay cut of nearly 50 per cent. I was only ever going to make one decision but, fortunately, I had met Denise, who was to become my wife. She was a very clever girl who earned more than I did, working as a computer programmer, which in 1970 was highly specialised work.

We were saving to buy our first house and with Denise's salary I could, ridiculous as it might sound today, afford to become a professional footballer. I signed the forms on her 21st birthday.

Valiant

(Games 1–236)

GORDON Lee was not given much of an inheritance when he took over at Port Vale. The club had been expelled from the Football League and was flooded with debt.

Because he had so little to work with, Gordon built a team of non-league players and free transfers, who were horrible to play against. We were tough, we were fit, we were strong. Nobody liked coming to Vale Park.

Just before he came to Hednesford to sign me, Gordon had won Port Vale promotion to the Third Division. Given what he had, it was a superb achievement.

His predecessor was the Potteries' greatest hero, Sir Stanley Matthews, who had been unable to transfer the brilliance of his play into management. In February 1968, the club pleaded guilty to making illegal payments to young footballers.

It was something a lot of clubs did but perhaps because Matthews was unconventional – he was vegetarian, teetotal, did not get on with authority and made a lot of money from advertising endorsements – they threw the book at Port Vale and expelled them.

It was overturned by a vote of Football League chairmen but when Gordon took over, Port Vale had an overdraft of £82,000, which in today's terms is around £1.3m.

I got to know Stanley Matthews, who despite playing more than 300 games for Stoke was a Port Vale fan. He was great friends with Reg Berks who was assistant manager at Port Vale and he also did some charity work with my brother, John.

I had watched him from the stands at Molineux when he played for Blackpool. When he played the game and when he talked about it, he was years ahead of his time.

Stanley Matthews played until he was 50 and, once I had become a professional footballer, one of my great fears was the call to come into the manager's office, where you might be told your time was up. I'd had that awful conversation in Ray Shaw's car when I was a teenager at Walsall and I never wanted to have it again.

The conversations I had with first Gordon Lee and then Roy Sproson, who took over from him in 1974, were about money rather than keeping my job. My wages increased every season by about five pounds a week until, by the time I left in 1976, I was being paid £60 a week. Inflation meant that in real terms I was actually being paid less than the £40 a week I had earned juggling non-league football and building work at Hednesford.

My best pal at Vale Park was a guy called Tommy McLaren. He was a Scotsman who had come to the club from Berwick, signed by Stanley Matthews. Tommy did not have the ability of George Best but in terms of looks and attitude there was something of Best about him. He could be a fabulous footballer.

He played on the right wing, he had long, black hair, all the girls loved him, even though he was married with two kids. I was amazed his career did not go further than Port Vale.

Tommy was a ferocious competitor. When he was playing a five-a-side he would tear into you. A few months after I had left to join Brighton, I went back to play Port Vale in a 2-2 draw in November 1976. As we were lining up to go out, Tommy turned and spat at my feet. He spat at my bloody feet. Then, as we ran out on to the pitch, he turned and winked at me. That was the way he was.

Less than two years later, Tommy was dead. He had split from his wife, Carol, they had two lovely kids and he was playing non-league football with Telford.

Port Vale had given him a free transfer after nine years – and you needed ten to qualify for a testimonial. I thought that was terrible treatment.

They found him dead in a garage in Telford and the assumption was he had committed suicide. I was convinced he would not have killed himself. He was too much of a fighter.

The story I heard was that Tommy had lost the keys to his house so he got into his car to spend the night in his garage, which he did have a key to. But it got cold, he turned on the engine to turn on the heater and fell asleep. The fumes got into the car and killed him. For years I would carry a photograph of Tommy McLaren in my wallet.

There were other strong friendships at Vale Park. John Brodie was an attacking right-back who should have played at a higher level.

Port Vale is in Burslem, in north Stoke, which was the very heart of the Potteries. Even in the 1970s, industry there was starting to decline and now there is very little of it left. People in Burslem tended to have it tough. They were lovely people but when they went to the football they expected to see some entertainment and at the very least some hard work for their money.

We were worked hard. The stand behind the goal at Vale Park used to be terracing that stretched to twice the height it is now. We would train by running up and down the terracing and, when that was done, we would be asked to do 15 laps of what was a very big pitch.

We would have lunch just by the ground at the Vale Café, which is still going. I'd have pie and chips. Always. Our other lunch venue was the Red Lion in Burslem, which was owned by Pete Conway, who is Robbie Williams's dad.

Because I lived in Cannock, I only trained with the rest of the team on Tuesday and Friday. The rest of the time I would train with Roy Cross, a centre-half, and the goalkeeper, Keith Ball, who lived in nearby Walsall. At that level in those days, some footballers would not have cars and Gordon Lee wanted to keep commuting to a minimum.

In my six years at Vale Park we scrapped and fought but only twice did we come close to promotion. We finished sixth in 1973 and 1975 but then there were no play-offs and we were always in the shadow of Stoke City.

Stoke had a fantastic side that included names such as Gordon Banks, Terry Conroy, Denis Smith, Jimmy Greenhoff, Mike Pejic and Geoff Hurst. In 1972 they beat Chelsea to win the League Cup and reached the FA Cup semi-final which was lost to Arsenal only after a replay. Had they won their last three games, Stoke, rather than Derby, would have won the league in 1975.

We would see the likes of Alan Hudson at certain nightclubs around the city such as The Place in Hanley or Place Mate in Newcastle-under-Lyme. The Place, which was in Bryan Street, claimed to be Britain's very first discotheque and at the start of their careers David Bowie, Rod Stewart, Elton John and Led Zeppelin all played there. I remember going to see Long John Baldry.

We would also take on Stoke at cricket every year, which was something Geoff Hurst enjoyed because he was a very good cricketer. He first met Bobby Moore when they were playing cricket for Essex Schools and Geoff went on to keep wicket for Essex Second XI.

I loved cricket. I batted and bowled and had a trial for Staffordshire Boys when I was at school. When I signed for Brighton, I used to watch the cricket at Hove whenever I could.

Sussex had an incredibly glamorous team – Tony Greig, Imran Khan, Javed Miandad and John Snow. In 1978 when Sussex won the Gillette Cup, Brighton played them at football and cricket.

Because there was so little money at Port Vale, because we were all free transfers, there was a real togetherness about the club. Ray Harford was our centre-half, although he would probably have admitted himself he was a better coach than he was a player. He was a lovely man who would manage Luton at Wembley and was Kenny Dalglish's number two when Blackburn won the Premier League.

In contrast to Stoke at the Victoria Ground, glamour was in short supply at Vale Park. There was a 4-4 draw with Aston Villa when they had fallen into the Third Division but the biggest occasion in my time at Port Vale was being drawn to play at home to West Ham in the FA Cup in January 1973.

West Ham had footballers with stardust, a team that would draw a crowd, footballers you would be desperate to pitch yourself against, knowing that at our level you might never face them again. Bobby Moore, Trevor Brooking, Frank Lampard Senior, Billy Bonds, Pop Robson, Clyde Best, Ted MacDougall. It was a game I missed.

A month before, we had been playing at The Valley. I was on the left wing, just about to cross a ball when a Charlton player came across and hit me, knee high. Bang. I knew something was wrong immediately.

In those days, you were allowed only one sub and Gordon Lee would not let me come off because he wouldn't allow Vale to go down to ten men. 'Just limp on up front,' he told me.

The Charlton club doctor saw me afterwards and, when we got back from London, the physio took me to the hospital in Stoke. When they examined the X-rays, I was told there was nothing substantially wrong.

I had treatment all week and played in the next game, at home to Scunthorpe, but when I came off after the match, I told the dressing room that something wasn't right.

The doctor sent me to another hospital, the Haywood near Vale Park, and when their X-rays came back, they showed a hairline fracture. The doctor went berserk and I missed the cup tie. West Ham won 1-0 in front of 20,600 which was then about four times Port Vale's average gate. I was furious and frustrated.

Gordon Lee left the club in 1974 to manage Blackburn, who were in the Third Division with Port Vale. He promoted them in his first season at Ewood Park and was then appointed manager of Newcastle.

On Tyneside he is remembered for selling Malcolm Macdonald and taking the club to the League Cup Final, which was lost to Manchester City. A year later Gordon would be back at Wembley with Everton in another League Cup Final. That, too, was lost.

Later he would say to me: 'I wish I'd taken you with me to Blackburn and Newcastle,' and I wish he had. Instead, I stayed at Port Vale under Roy Sproson, who played more than 800 times for the club and whose statue is outside Vale Park. I was 26, then 27 and I wondered if my professional career would go any further than Burslem.

I certainly followed the transfer gossip and had become friends with John Maddock, a journalist who worked for *The Sunday People*, where he and Norman Wynne seemed to have the inside track on what was happening in the game.

John was good friends with Reg Berks, who was not only Port Vale's assistant manager but also ran a pub. Roy Sproson was far too much of a gentleman to give anyone a bollocking and Reg was the shouter and the bawler in the Vale Park dressing room.

One summer, Port Vale organised a tour to Malta. One of the staff couldn't make it and Reg asked John if he would like to come. The players were pretty unhappy because one thing they did not want was a journalist in the hotel, printing tales of what they might be getting up to away from home.

John said he would not report anything and he was as good as his word but we decided to treat him as we would any other new boy on tour by playing a practical joke. When he came back to his room after a night out, it was to find his bed on the hotel balcony.

In the days before agents got a grip of the game, John Maddock and journalists like him were very powerful people because of who they knew. John would help Mark Lawrenson get the manager's job at Oxford United because it was owned by Robert Maxwell, who ran *The Sunday People*.

John, who was close to Alex Ferguson, was the go-between when Ron Atkinson got the Manchester United job and he was instrumental in me coming to Manchester City because by then he was the club's general manager.

One thing was certain. When Port Vale travelled down to play Crystal Palace in March 1976, John Maddock would have known I was to be sold that night. It was not just John who was in the know; everyone on that Port Vale bus travelling south to London seemed to know this would be my last game. Everyone except me.

Seagull Special

(Games 237–454)

'**W**HAT is it you like, Brian? Do you drink? Do you like women? Do you gamble?'

It was gone midnight. I was in Peter Taylor's suite at the Metropole Hotel on Brighton's seafront. A few hours before I'd been at Selhurst Park, playing for Port Vale against Crystal Palace. Now, here I was listening to one half of the great managerial partnership of Clough and Taylor probe for a weakness. I told him I'd have a beer.

It was a Tuesday night in March 1976, my 236th and last game for Port Vale. After the 2-2 draw, the manager, Roy Sproson, took me to one side and told me the club needed £30,000 and I was to be sold to Brighton.

If I were going to be transferred, I half-imagined I'd be joining Crystal Palace, who were managed by Malcolm Allison with Terry Venables as his assistant. That season they would reach the semi-finals of the FA Cup and before the game one of Palace's backroom staff had said to me: 'Don't do anything stupid and we'll see you back here.'

Roy said there was a car waiting outside to take me to Brighton. I had to phone my wife to tell her I wouldn't be coming home. As I walked out of Selhurst Park to find a limousine – a big Ford Granada – and a driver, it occurred to me I had no change of clothing, just the tracksuit I was wearing.

We arrived at the Metropole and I was shown to Peter Taylor's suite, where there was football playing on the television. It was then that he asked me if I wanted a drink and then, if there was anything else I fancied. I found out later that this was a tactic Taylor employed with every potential signing. Did they have a weakness for 'booze, birds or betting'? He liked to know in advance.

That Peter Taylor was at Brighton at all was extraordinary. In October 1973 he and Brian Clough had walked out of Derby six months after taking them to a European Cup semi-final and 18 months after winning them the league.

Mike Bamber was Brighton's chairman, a property developer in his forties. He wanted to spend his money on the club and he knew the value of publicity. He offered Clough and Taylor more money than they had earned at Derby to manage in the Third Division.

By the time the limousine pulled up outside the Metropole, Clough had long gone. Taylor said Brian's heart had never been in the job. He had not moved down to Sussex and he had hankered after a return to the First Division. When Leeds hired him to replace Don Revie in the summer of 1974, Taylor had stayed.

He was a big man; he'd been a goalkeeper. At Derby and at Nottingham Forest he was the one who scouted the players and sorted the transfers. He had watched me when Port Vale had played Rotherham and, unlike most managers, he did not go into the directors' box to watch a game. He would pay at the gate, stand behind the goal or watch from the sides.

I had been captain of Port Vale and he said he would make me captain of Brighton straight away. My wages at Port Vale had been £60 a week and Taylor offered me £100, which in 1976 was considered decent money. It would be worth seven times that today.

I watched them play Shrewsbury at the Goldstone Ground and afterwards I saw Taylor and asked if I could have a bit more than £100?

'That's your offer,' he said. 'If you don't like it, I'll put you on the next train back home.'

I told him I'd take the £100.

He was under pressure. We were going for promotion but results were starting to falter and on a Wednesday night, after we had lost at Chesterfield, he went over to four players in the dressing room, pointed at them and said: 'You will never play for me again.'

Two days later, at a team meeting, when he'd had a chance to calm down, Taylor pointed to the same four players and told them exactly the same thing. They would never play for him again. He had signed them all. When we lost at Millwall on Easter Monday, it was something from which we didn't really recover.

I played only 12 games for Peter Taylor and I wish there had been more but he was shaken by Brighton's failure to reach the Second Division, although as players we had no inkling he would quit.

After the final game of the season, a 1-1 draw at home to Sheffield Wednesday, we went off to an Italian restaurant and then Peter went with us on a post-season break to Torremolinos.

Taylor stayed on in Spain. He had a house in Majorca and it was there that he met Brian Clough who persuaded Peter to join him at Nottingham Forest. I think you know the rest.

One of Peter Taylor's legacies to Brighton was Peter Ward, whom he had signed from Burton for £4,000. He would become one of the club's finest strikers.

He was a cocky little bugger who was a long way from the hardest-working man at the club but who finished like few others ever could in a Brighton shirt. He scored in the first minute of his debut against Hereford, which unusually for a Third Division fixture was televised by *Match of the Day*. The fans adored him.

His first strike partner at the club was Ian Mellor, the father of Neil Mellor, who would play for Liverpool. One of their first games together was against Walsall. Because I had been released by Walsall when I was 17 and because my mum was from the town, it was a fixture I always relished, although at Port Vale we could never seem to beat them.

It was a rain-drenched Tuesday night in October 1976. It was goalless at half-time and Alan Mullery, who had replaced Taylor as manager, sent us out of the dressing room after about a minute to wait in the rain for the restart. Brighton scored seven times in the second half. Ward scored four, Mellor scored three. In that season, his first full one at the Goldstone, Wardy scored 36 times, beating the club record which had stood since 1933. It rather annoyed him that I was voted Brighton's player of the season.

We shared the penalty-taking duties until the final home game of the season. Once more we were playing Sheffield Wednesday at the Goldstone Ground, this time in front of more than 30,000. If Brighton won, we would be promoted.

Wednesday took the lead, Brighton equalised and then Wardy screwed a penalty wide. Brighton were then awarded another penalty and I asked Peter if he wanted to take it but he just shook his head. The pressure had got to him. I took it and scored. Brighton won, 3-2. Afterwards, I told him in pretty harsh language that in future I would take the penalties.

That morning I had woken up feeling dreadful and rang the club doctor, Herzl Sless. Peter O'Sullivan, who played left midfield, also complained of the same symptoms. Dr Sless told us to go to the Metropole and stay in the same room so we didn't infect anyone else.

Before the game he came over to give us an injection which got us through the match, although after the final whistle when all the talk was about going out to celebrate, I felt awful again and went home. A couple of days later, I asked Dr Sless what he had injected us with. He said, 'water'.

On the pitch I was on Peter Ward's back all the time. He would dribble when he might have passed. He could be selfish but he was a kid with tremendous talent. When I was at Luton, Paul Walsh was the same. His dad would come over after the game and say: 'You keep on at him, it's the only way he's going to learn.'

Wardy benefited from having Teddy Maybank alongside him. When he came to Brighton from Fulham, Teddy was the club's record signing – his transfer paid for the Eric Miller Stand at Craven Cottage. Although he did not get the goals or the headlines that Peter did, Teddy was a fantastic influence on and off the pitch. Away from the Goldstone Ground, Teddy liked a good time and Brighton under Mike Bamber was a club that had plenty of good times. To this day we still keep in touch.

Wardy was a fine player, who might have done even better had his transfer to Nottingham Forest worked out. Peter Taylor brought him to the City Ground in October 1980 for £400,000 which was 100 times more than Brighton had paid for him. By then Forest were double European champions.

The relationship between Clough and Taylor was that Peter scouted and bought the players but there were one or two that Brian took an instant aversion to and Ward was one of them. Taylor said that the signing of Peter Ward was the first time Clough openly questioned his judgement. Generally, at Forest, if Brian didn't like you, you were gone.

For most of my time at Brighton, the judgements that mattered were those made by Alan Mullery.

Alan was 34 when he came to the Goldstone Ground. He was a star, who had played for England in the World Cup in Mexico and won the FA Cup and the UEFA Cup with Tottenham. The year before he became Brighton manager, he, Bobby Moore and Rodney Marsh had taken Fulham to the FA Cup Final.

He says that a couple of years earlier, when Fulham were playing Brighton, Mike Bamber had been impressed by the sight of him punching one of his own players who had been at fault for a goal. He now offered him the chance to succeed Peter Taylor.

What worried me was that he played in my position and when we played a training game, an eight v eight or a six v six, he was invariably the best player. For some reason, we were never on the same side during those training games and, if his team was losing, those games seemed to go on for hours. If he was winning, the gaffer would blow the whistle.

However, once he came to Brighton, Alan considered himself solely a manager. He took Brighton from the Third to the First Division and gave the club some of their greatest days.

He could be hard, ruthless. He had a saying: 'I will tell you once, I will tell you twice.' There would not be a third time. He would just get rid.

One of my earliest memories of him was coming back on the coach from Grimsby. We had started the season well and this had been our first defeat but I had been sent off and we had missed a penalty.

In the dressing room at Blundell Park, he screamed at everyone in general and me in particular and then refused to speak a word to any of us on the bus back – and it is a long way from Grimsby to Brighton. Sometimes, the only sign he was pleased with you was if he tossed you a cigar as we were travelling back on the coach or the train.

When Alan Mullery came to Brighton, he bought with him Ken Craggs as his number two. Part of his job was to pick us up off the floor after we had received our bollockings from the manager.

They were a great partnership. Ken had come down from County Durham with Bobby Robson to play for Fulham. He loved a cigarette, loved a bet and loved being with the players. He would scout for me at Hull, Oxford and Manchester City. He became Brighton's chief scout when I returned to the south coast to manage.

Travelling was the biggest difference I noticed when I joined Brighton. At Port Vale we would generally not have a pre-match meal. We would get on the coach, play the game and, if we had got a result, we would be allowed ten bob to buy a sandwich from a motorway service station. At Brighton, we travelled first class, we stayed in hotels and the club had a sponsorship with British Caledonian that allowed us to fly to away games in the north.

When I came to Brighton, I had just bought a Ford Capri and I used to take it to a garage in the town called The Endeavour. One day they asked if I'd like to drive around in a sponsored Capri. It had a registration 444V because I wore the number four shirt. One summer they asked if I fancied driving a Ford Mustang around town for a few months. The answer was yes.

There were other cars on offer. Mark Lawrenson had a sporty little Triumph. Alan Mullery had a Jaguar. Peter Ward had been the first to get a sponsored car, a Rover 2.6.

The players called a meeting demanding to know why we had been given cars and the rest of them hadn't. Mullery walked into the meeting and began pointing at the players saying to each of them: 'Who are you?' and when they tried to reply, he added: 'Why would anyone want to sponsor you?'

He told them: 'Brian Horton has a car because he is captain of this football club. Mark Lawrenson is the best player. Peter Ward scored almost 40 goals last season and I am the manager. If the rest of you can't get sponsored cars, that's your problem.' With that, he left.

As captain I had to put the concerns of the players to the manager, which was something Mullery hated. He thought that as captain I should have been able to sort these things out. That I had to come to him was, in his eyes, a sign of weakness.

He lived in Surrey in a beautiful house that backed on to the golf course at Cheam and he invited me to a party he was hosting there. Naturally, I was ribbed mercilessly about 'sucking up to the gaffer' to the extent that I told Alan I would rather not go. Mullery was astonished I should have paid any attention to what the players had said. He considered their thoughts irrelevant. I went to the party.

That attitude extended to the pitch. He thought everyone in his dressing room should know their own game. He may have played in a World Cup but Alan Mullery was not one for giving advice.

That way of thinking was not unusual among managers at the time. When Graeme Souness moved from a provincial club like Middlesbrough to Liverpool, who had just retained the European Cup, he asked Bob Paisley how he wanted him to adjust his game now he was at Anfield. It was an intelligent question but Paisley looked at Souness as if he were mad. Alan Mullery's attitude was the same – the player should sort it out himself.

It was in Alan Mullery's first season that the rivalry between Brighton and Crystal Palace grew bitter. Crystal Palace were managed by Terry Venables and, although they had been team-mates at Tottenham, he and Mullery grated on each other.

In November 1976, Brighton and Palace drew each other in the first round of the FA Cup. The first two games, at the Goldstone Ground then at Selhurst Park, were drawn. A second replay was staged at Stamford Bridge.

Brighton were a goal down when the referee, Ron Challis, awarded us a penalty. I scored but Challis ordered it to be retaken because he had spotted an encroachment because one of Crystal Palace's players had pushed Peter Ward into the area. I promptly missed the second penalty and we were knocked out.

Mullery went mad at the final whistle and had a go at Ron Challis, for which he was charged by the FA. As he made to go down the tunnel, some Crystal Palace fans spat at him. Alan gave them two fingers and then gave an interview saying he wouldn't give five pounds for the whole of that Palace team. Ron Challis had to leave Stamford Bridge under police protection. Six years later, Alan accepted an offer from Crystal Palace to become their manager, which strange to say, didn't really work out.

The summer of 1977 was the one in which Brighton bought Mark Lawrenson. I was at Hove Park playing tennis with Steve Piper – who had been a major part of the Brighton defence for the last five years. We went back to the ground for a shower and saw the gaffer.

Alan was smoking a cigar which is something he did when he was making 'announcements'. He said: 'I have just bought the best centre-half in the Third Division.'

I went through a few names and he said: 'Mark Lawrenson.' Lawrenson didn't register with me. We'd beaten Preston easily; Lawrenson was a teenager who hadn't impressed against Peter Ward. I said: 'Are you sure?'

Mullery had paid £100,000 for Lawrenson and in doing so a club that had just won promotion to the Second Division had outbid Liverpool, who were then European champions.

Mark was a superb defender despite being one of the worst trainers I have ever known.

He was utterly casual, completely laid back. If you were staging an eight v eight in training, Lawro would be last pick. On the training ground he would go through the motions. He would be the last to get changed on a Saturday afternoon. He would come in at 25 to three, holding a cup of tea after Alan Mullery had been demanding to know where he had been. He would then perform beautifully.

We became great friends. He told me that when he went to Liverpool he had to become more disciplined off the pitch. Players like Dalglish and Souness would not tolerate lateness, let alone the management.

A couple of years later, Mullery signed another centre-half who was to become one of Brighton's best-loved players. Steve Foster wore a headband not because he wanted to make a fashion statement but because he wanted to protect the scar tissue on his forehead. He had split his head open in a challenge with Andy Gray and the wound would open up if he clashed heads again.

Later in his career, Fozzie had headbands ready-made but in the early days at Brighton the kit man would make them from cut-up white towels which he would stick on to Steve's head with Velcro.

Fozzie and I became room-mates on away trips. We were similar characters; we were competitive, we liked a drink, we liked a bet and once we put on the shirt we liked to win.

He wasn't given the respect he deserved. Perhaps it was the headband but he was portrayed as a hulking header of the ball. In fact, he had begun his career at Portsmouth as a centre-forward until Ian St John converted him into a centre-half who was very good with the ball at his feet. He played in three Wembley finals and went with England to the 1982 World Cup where he shared a room with Glenn Hoddle.

He was a good talker in the dressing room and sometimes you needed someone other than the manager to address the players. They sometimes needed to hear a different voice.

Fozzie was part of a wonderful team spirit that Brighton nurtured. Mike Bamber had a housing development near Hove Park and it became a little community for Brighton's footballers. When Peter Ward was sold to Nottingham Forest, I asked the chairman if I could have his house. Gordon Smith lived nearby and so did Lawro. We used to walk the dogs together. I had a golden retriever; Mark had an old English sheepdog – a Dulux dog.

Every season with Brighton seemed to go to the wire. We won promotion to the Second Division in 1977. However, it rankled with Alan that we didn't go up as champions but the Sheffield Wednesday game was the only one of our last four that we won. Mansfield won the league and Crystal Palace were promoted with us.

That was nothing compared to Mullery's disappointment the following season. There were by now some very big clubs in the Second Division. Tottenham, Southampton, who had won the FA Cup two years before, and Sunderland, who like Spurs had just been relegated.

The league was won by Bolton and two from three – Brighton, Southampton and Spurs – would join them in the top flight. It went down to the last Saturday of the season. Tottenham and Southampton played each other at The Dell. Brighton were fourth, one point below Spurs.

Southampton and Tottenham had a much better goal difference than Brighton so we needed to beat Blackpool at the Goldstone Ground and hope Southampton beat Spurs.

The atmosphere at the Goldstone would be remembered by anyone who was there. It was jammed and as loud as it had ever been. We won, 2-1, and in doing so relegated Blackpool.

Further along the south coast, two teams who that season had scored 146 goals between them appeared to be doing their best not to find the net.

Just before the end, we heard a roar across the Goldstone and we thought Southampton had scored. In fact, it was the reaction to Alan Ball striking the frame of the goal. When the final whistle went, there was the realisation that the 0-0 draw at The Dell had sent Tottenham up on goal difference. People were in tears.

The atmosphere in the dressing room was shocking, mostly because we thought this was our chance of playing top-flight football and it would never come again. I was 29. It seemed doubtful, even though Alan Mullery grabbed a microphone and promised the crowd promotion next season.

A year later, we kept the promise, promoted alongside Crystal Palace and Stoke. For the first time in their history, Brighton and Hove Albion were a top-flight club.

The final afternoon of the season arrived with Brighton in second place, level on points with Stoke, one behind Crystal Palace and one ahead of Sunderland who were in fourth. Palace were the only ones at home. Stoke were at Notts County, Sunderland were at Wrexham and we were at Newcastle. We were, however, without Mark Lawrenson, who had broken his arm.

For a Saturday game, we travelled to the North East on the Wednesday staying at the Posthouse at Washington. Newcastle were mid-table but Mullery took us to St James' Park to see them beat Bristol Rovers. He wanted us to see Newcastle win, he wanted us to know we would have it hard.

Newcastle had nothing to play for and there was a lot of talk on Tyneside that they would let us win to keep Sunderland down. Mullery wanted none of those conversations in our dressing room.

Sunderland had let us use their training ground which was astonishingly good of them considering they needed us to lose. Thursday was the general election that saw Margaret Thatcher become Britain's first woman prime minister.

I asked Alan if we could play golf. Usually, the refusal would be immediate. The rule was that you never played golf after Wednesday if there was a Saturday game. This time he said yes, provided there was no booze involved. We played at Gosforth Park.

Mullery wanted us relaxed and it worked to the extent that at half-time at St James' Park we were 3-0 up. I'd opened the scoring with a header from Gary Williams's cross. Peter Ward scored the second and Gerry Ryan put the third away after a lovely move.

There were about 10,000 fans from Brighton packed into the Leazes End of St James' Park. The game had been played in sunshine, snow and rain and when the whistle went, Brighton had been promoted to the First Division for the first time in their history.

A large proportion of those fans had travelled on a chartered train called The Seagull Special which was used to take supporters to some away games. We went back to Brighton with them and we must have drunk that train dry. We went through every carriage to celebrate with the fans.

When I first went to Brighton people told me it was 'not a football town' and that I wouldn't get on with 'southern people'. The town was lively, passionate, lovely. I got on very well with southern people.

In my first full season, in the Third Division, the average attendance at the Goldstone Ground was 20,000 – more than Leicester, Nottingham Forest, Stoke or the two Sheffield clubs. In that weekend in May 1979 it seemed like the biggest football town in the country. The social life was fabulous. We'd go horse-racing at Fontwell where we'd meet Mick Channon and Alan Ball, who were with Southampton. Bamber called me 'capitano'.

'Everything okay capitano?

'We could do with a golf day chairman.'

'You organise it, I'll pay for it and don't forget to make sure the directors and manager are involved.'

He treated the players like kings. There would always be a post-season trip abroad.

In the promotion summer of 1979 Mike Bamber arranged for us all to go to the United States – which was unusual – and we could take our wives, which was even more unusual.

Bamber had business contacts in America and used them on Brighton's behalf. In San Diego, we played California Surf, who George Graham turned out for. Mullery told everyone to take it easy because it was a friendly and then managed to get himself sent off.

The North American Soccer League, which had seen Pele, Bobby Moore and Franz Beckenbauer play in the United States, was now in serious financial trouble and our next opponents, Las Vegas Seagulls, had just folded.

We had driven through the desert from San Diego to Las Vegas and the fact our opponents had gone bankrupt didn't stop us going to the Strip. We stayed at the Riviera, a casino with more than 2,000 rooms attached which like many things in Las Vegas was owned by the Mob. The original *Ocean's Eleven* and *Diamonds are Forever* had been filmed there. We may not have played any football but we saw Tony Bennett and Shirley MacLaine. Mike Bamber had insisted that everything be charged to the club.

The directors, especially Harry Bloom who was the grandfather of Brighton's current chairman, Tony Bloom, travelled with the team for games or for golf days. It felt like a family. They would play cards with the manager in the front of the coach or the train, they would stay with us in the hotel on a Friday night.

That sense of family lasted long after I left Brighton. I still speak to Ken Craggs and his wife, Angela, and am in regular contact with Alan Mullery and his wife Jean.

In April 1980, we were playing Stoke at the Victoria Ground. Denise, my wife, had parents in Stafford, mine were in Cannock, so for games at Stoke we'd go up to see them on the proviso I would be at the hotel, the Posthouse in Stoke, an hour before the team arrived.

Mark Lawrenson came into the foyer and whispered: 'Have you heard about Harry Bloom? Mr Bloom has died on the team coach.' He would always sit next to Mike Bamber and had been playing cards when he suffered a heart attack.

Harry had been vice-chairman of the club and had been a buffer between Mike Bamber and Alan Mullery. After his death the relationship between chairman and manager began to corrode.

In the summer of 1979, I came to him over the subject of bonuses. We had just won promotion to the First Division and the players were unhappy about the money they were being offered. In his autobiography, Alan says we threatened to strike and that for Brighton's first game in the top flight, against Arsenal, he threatened to dump us all and play the kids.

The threat to drop everyone may have been real but I am not sure we were actually about to join a picket line. Nevertheless, it affected our preparations and we were thrashed 4-0 at the Goldstone Ground by a team whose last competitive game had seen them win the FA Cup. We lost four of our opening five matches. By November we were bottom.

The turning point was against Nottingham Forest at the City Ground, where they had not lost a league game in 42 matches spanning two-and-a-half years. They could have won this one by ten. Mark Lawrenson played in midfield alongside me and we were completely overrun. John Robertson had a penalty saved. They murdered us. We had one chance and scored.

Brian Clough was gracious in defeat and came into our dressing room to offer his congratulations. He wasn't quite so gracious a few months later at the Goldstone Ground when Brighton did the double over them. Gary Williams was a defender who came from Preston in the Mark Lawrenson deal and he had a fearsome shot. This time he used it to beat Peter Shilton from 30 yards. Clough was furious and claimed Brighton had won with a fluke.

In 1980 Brighton finished 16th, ahead of Manchester City and Everton. Derby, who five years before had been league champions, were relegated.

The following season climaxed with one of the most extraordinary escapes in the history of the First Division. With five games to go, Crystal Palace were doomed at the foot of the table and Brighton looked likeliest to be relegated with them.

The first of our five remaining games was at Middlesbrough. We could not have played any worse if you'd asked us to. The sole positive was that Middlesbrough only won 1-0.

On the Monday morning Mullery told me to gather the players for a meeting upstairs at the Goldstone. Unbelievably, for a club that was in the top flight of English football, Brighton did not have a training ground.

We would either train at Hove Park, in between the trees, or we would go out in the middle of Hove dog track, which wasn't big enough to hold a football pitch.

We all climbed the stairs to the meeting room to find not only Alan Mullery but Mike Bamber. Mullery started with me: 'You're the captain of this football club. What's your opinion about Saturday?'

Before I could speak, he said: 'You don't fucking tackle anybody any more. You are not committed any more.' He slaughtered me.

Then he turned to Steve Foster. 'You, with your fucking headband, what do you think?' Again, before Steve could utter a word, Mullery exploded: 'You can't tackle either and you can't win a header.'

Mark Lawrenson was next. 'You're the superstar in this team, what do you think?'

Mark paused, thought about it and said: 'Do you think we're not good enough, gaffer?'

At this Mullery went berserk. 'Not good enough? I have signed every one of you fucking players except Nobby Horton and you have the nerve to tell me we are not good enough.'

Then, he turned to Gary Stevens who was only 19. We used to call him 'Grease' because he had black hair done in a quiff like John Travolta.

'I think we could try a bit harder, gaffer.'

'Spot on. You are not trying.' Then he added, pointing to us all: 'If I ever saw you lot in the street, I would run you over.'

At the back of the room, Mike Bamber piped up: 'And so would I.'

We had four games left. We were third from bottom with 27 points, two fewer than Norwich who were just above the relegation line. The first three would be against teams in or around the drop zone. Wins would count for plenty; defeats would be doubly damaging.

The first was at Selhurst Park, against an already-doomed Crystal Palace. We won, 3-0. John Gregory scored twice. On Easter Monday we played Leicester, who were now just below us, at the Goldstone Ground. We were 1-0 down at half-time but John Gregory and Michael Robinson scored to give us the win.

Those victories, however, did us little good. Norwich had beaten Tottenham at White Hart Lane and won the East Anglian derby against Ipswich, who that season would win the UEFA Cup.

We had to travel to Sunderland, who having lost four of their last five, were now serious candidates for the drop. Brighton's sponsorship deal with British Caledonian meant we could fly up to the North East.

It was 1-1 and time was slipping away. Roker Park was loud and packed. A draw suited them far more than it did us and then in the 89th minute, Gary Williams once more unleashed a fearsome shot that this time crashed into the back of the Sunderland net. The silence at Roker was like a shroud. Brighton were clear of the relegation zone on goal difference.

The final Saturday of the season dawned with Crystal Palace and Leicester relegated. One from Brighton, Norwich and Sunderland would join them. All had 33 points. Norwich, who had the worst goal difference, had the easiest fixture, at home to Leicester. Sunderland were at Anfield, where they had not won since 1936. We had Leeds at the Goldstone Ground.

We won 2-0. Steve Foster scored the first, Andy Ritchie the second. The other results were more remarkable. At Carrow Road, Norwich lost to Leicester, 3-2, while on Merseyside, Sunderland, playing a team preparing for a European Cup Final against Real Madrid, beat Liverpool.

The mood was euphoric but for Alan Mullery and myself it would be the end.

A few weeks later, I was in the garden sunbathing when there was knock on the door. It was Alan. He told me he had just resigned as Brighton's manager.

Mullery never enjoyed the relationship with Mike Bamber that the players did. While Harry Bloom was alive, it was tolerable. After Harry's death it fell apart.

Despite Brighton's success, attendances at the Goldstone Ground were tailing off. The average attendance in the 1980/81 season – our second in the top flight – was 18,900, which was less than it had been when we won promotion from the Third Division in 1977. A combination of recession, unemployment and hooliganism had all played their part.

Mark Lawrenson was the club's most saleable asset and Alan Mullery thought he had struck a deal to sell him to Manchester United for £400,000 plus two players. It was complicated by the fact that Ron Atkinson had only just taken up his position at Old Trafford.

Liverpool offered a straight cash deal of £900,000 for Mark and it was this deal that Mike Bamber accepted, without telling his manager. It was something Alan could not stomach.

He stood at the door: 'I've resigned and I'll tell you something else, they want to sell you, too.' I was 32, there was a year left on my contract. Alan thanked me for what I'd done for him at Brighton and, as he turned to go, I reminded him that he'd once threatened to run me over.

'Yes,' he said. 'But it was good motivation, wasn't it?'

Alan Mullery (manager, Brighton and Hove Albion 1976–1981)

When I arrived to manage Brighton I didn't have a clue who Brian Horton was. I had never watched the lower divisions but the day after I was appointed manager, I found out what he was.

I took a session on the pitches at Brighton College and I asked Ken Gutteridge, who was then the assistant manager, to organise a match between the team that had just missed out on promotion under Peter Taylor and the rest of the squad.

When I saw Brian play, I thought: 'I am never going to play football again.' He played in my position and shone so much on leadership and determination that I warmed to him immediately. I said to Ken: 'Who is this fella?'

Ken said: 'That's the captain. Peter bought him from Port Vale.'

He was just like me. I did exactly the same things Brian did. I was 34 and I could have been Brighton's player-manager but, having seen what Brian could do, I realised I could concentrate on just managing the team and I already had a captain. That was after 30 minutes of watching him in a friendly.

The training facilities at Brighton were fairly basic. What used to get me down was that when we went to the local park to train, we would be treading in dog shit. I asked myself if this was really how it was in the Third Division and told myself I just had to get on with it.

The Goldstone Ground itself was a tip with seagull droppings all over the place and a pitch which had a slope on it. The dressing rooms were poor and yet Brighton could get 30,000 crowds. It was amazing.

Peter Taylor had left me with a decent squad. I think Brian Clough had just played at being manager at Brighton but Peter had been very committed. I inherited Brian and Peter Ward, who began scoring goals in a way he had never done before.

I said to Brian: 'When you are on the pitch, you are the manager but, if you make decisions that are wrong, I will give you the biggest bollocking you have ever had in your life.' Most of the decisions he made were right.

The role of a captain was one I really valued. I had been captain at Tottenham for five years. At Fulham I captained Bobby Moore, who had been captain of England for most of his career.

There is one game at Brighton that really stands out. It wasn't one of the big ones but it was on a wet Wednesday night at home to Walsall in 1976. The first half was appalling. We kept going down their end before giving the ball to them and they went down our end before giving the ball to us. This went on for 45 minutes.

When we got into the dressing room for half-time there was always a tray with cups of tea laid out for us. I threw it into the air and told the players to go back out on to the pitch and stand in the rain. I said: 'The public out there are getting soaking wet and you are not doing anything for them so get your arses out there and stand with them.' In the opening 25 minutes of the second half we scored seven goals.

What struck me when we got into the big league was how much money Brighton spent in the summer of 1979 – £3m. We signed people like Michael Robinson, Andy Ritchie, John Gregory. For the time it was an enormous amount.

I always wanted to find out what made our players tick. The one I never really got close to was Stevie Foster. He was a terrific player but he was a very quiet lad, a bit of a ducker and diver but a rock on the pitch.

Mark Lawrenson had an attitude that I found hard to fathom. I would sometimes give him bollockings about being late or his performances in training, pointing out that even though he was a very, very good player, he was taking the piss out of his team-mates. I wouldn't do it in front of the team. I would take him to one side.

Then, when the game kicked off, you would forgive Mark everything. He was like a Ferrari that would just sit there on the drive forever and then, when somebody got in it, would roar off.

Brian's attitude was totally the opposite. When we had five-a-sides on a Thursday, he would turn on people as if it were a real match. I used to yell at him from the sidelines: 'We've got a game at the weekend; you are killing three or four of our players.' However, it was precisely the attitude I wanted.

I was young when I took over at Brighton and it was my first job in management. I would speak to Bill Nicholson at least once a week. He had retired from management, although he was still doing some scouting for Tottenham. He was a miserable, dour Yorkshireman but he was also one of the greatest and most innovative managers this country has ever had. At Tottenham, they were doing things under Bill that they are still doing now.

I would ask Bill his advice on what was going on at the club, if he had any recommendations for players and I would go through our training routines to see if he had any suggestions.

The job came to an end over Lawro. The top four sides in the First Division would phone me regularly to ask if Lawrenson was available. The answer would always be no.

Then one Wednesday Mike Bamber came in to see me and said: 'I need 400 grand to pay the bank off.'

I replied: 'Okay, I will sell Mark Lawrenson.'

'Really?'

'Yes, if we need the money and it will benefit the club, I will sell him.'

Liverpool and Manchester United both wanted him and I wanted a million pounds for him.

Then one day, I found out he had been sold behind my back. I went to see the chairman to ask why he had done it.

He said: 'To tell you the truth, there are stacks of millionaires in Brighton and I am one of them but none of those millionaires have sold a player for a million pounds.'

I looked at him and his wife and shook him by the hand and said: 'I suppose you are going to pick the team now?'

He replied: 'I have been thinking about that.'

That was me done at Brighton.

Mark Lawrenson (Brighton and Hove Albion 1977–1981)

I came to Brighton in a bit of a daze, so much so that I nearly failed my medical. I had been with Preston on an end-of-season trip to Spain and was signed by Brighton in a café in Benidorm. Miami Mike (Bamber) and Dudley Sizen, who was on the board, came over to do the deal.

I signed a blank contract and my stepfather, who was a director at Preston, agreed the money over the phone from Lytham St Anne's.

When I got to Brighton for my medical, they thought I was a diabetic. Dr Sless, the club doctor, asked me all sorts of questions and then carried out a series of blood tests and at four o'clock in the afternoon he said: 'I am sorry, this cannot go through.'

When he asked where I'd been, I told him I'd been out in Spain with the lads. He said: 'Have you been drinking alcohol?'

'Guinness, all week.'

'That shouldn't be a problem. Did you have anything else?'

'I drink Guinness with blackcurrant.'

'How much blackcurrant?'

'A lot.'

I'd drunk so much that it had affected my blood sugar levels.

Brian was our manager on the pitch and, if he had possessed a bit of pace, he would have played at the very highest level and on a regular basis. The type of player he was no longer exists.

He had this stare. He would just have to look at you to tell you that you needed to do better. He was also very big on team spirit. There were very few homegrown players at Brighton and the dressing room had a lot of players who had come to the south coast for the first time and needed bringing together.

Every time we came back from an away game, we all used to go to a pub called Hove Place and the rule was that everyone had to come in for one drink – it didn't have to be alcohol but they had to come in. Friday lunchtimes we would meet in a restaurant in The Lanes called Al Forno's.

It was a vibrant club and at that time there was a real buzz around the town, a feeling that we were going somewhere. I had broken my arm before we went up to play Newcastle in the game that would see us promoted to the top flight. I was sat next to Miami Mike watching the game, which we cruised, and afterwards I tried to get on to the pitch at St James' Park to celebrate with the rest of the team. A policeman thought I was a punter and tried to arrest me for attempting to invade the pitch.

Hatter

(Games 455–572)

'I'M not interested in what you've done. You have to prove yourself to me.' I was talking to Brighton's new manager, Mike Bailey. Alan Mullery had been right. They did want me out.

I was absolutely staggered at what I was hearing. 'You're telling me I need to prove myself. I have captained this club from the Third to the First Division. I have no need to prove myself to anyone.'

There was little use protesting. Bailey's mind was made up. He informed me I would be stripped of the captaincy if I tried to stay.

Brighton had been involved with a straight swap with Charlton who had just won promotion to the Second Division. Bailey went to the Goldstone Ground while Mullery dropped down a division to go to The Valley.

He had been linked with West Bromwich Albion who needed a manager now that Ron Atkinson had gone to

Manchester United but he lived in Surrey and Charlton would have been more convenient.

I often wonder what would have happened had Alan Mullery not quit Brighton. I did want to stay. I loved Brighton, the place, the people and its football club.

Alan knew I was interested in coaching and I am sure I would have earned a place on his backroom team. Perhaps I might have succeeded him as manager. I certainly thought I could have seen out my career at the Goldstone Ground.

I had an accountant, Colin Brennan, who was something of an adviser to me. Colin was unmistakable, six feet seven tall, a huge Brighton fan and a very good golfer. Most players then didn't have agents but I turned to Colin whenever I needed financial, career or even golf advice.

Colin pointed out that, since I had a year remaining on my contract, I still had some leverage with the club and I arranged to meet the chairman, Mike Bamber, once he'd come back from holiday.

I went to see him in the new offices they'd had built in Hove in the hope he might put some pressure on Mike Bailey. 'I am going to have to back my manager,' he said. Bamber did not want to be seen to be interfering in team affairs but he agreed to pay up the remaining year of my contract. I left his office with a cheque but no job.

It was probably the best thing that ever happened to me; not because I left a town and a club that I adored but because I met a man who was to become the biggest influence on my life.

David Pleat was completely different to Alan Mullery. Alan's managerial ethos was to buy good players and motivate them. He had played for England in a World Cup. He dominated a dressing room. David was a coach. He talked to you, he explained why he wanted you to do something. He didn't rant.

David had played for England Schoolboys and, had he not suffered a serious injury when he was a teenager at Nottingham Forest, he could have enjoyed a very good playing career. He played for Luton Town and Exeter and managed Nuneaton but it was when he came back to Kenilworth Road in 1978 that his career as a manager really took off.

David kept Luton in the Second Division and then pushed them upwards. They finished sixth in 1980 with a few less points than Chelsea and a few more than West Ham and Newcastle. A year later they were fifth. These days both seasons would have seen them in the play-offs.

I came to replace Alan West who had gone to Millwall while Paul Price went to Tottenham for £250,000. That was the only transfer business Luton did in the summer of 1981. By the following May they had won the Second Division with 88 points and were back in top-flight football.

I noticed the difference with David Pleat the moment we started pre-season training. Then, pre-season was all about fitness; summers seemed to be spent in endless rounds of cross-country running. At Luton, we tended to use a football. We went on a tour of Sweden, playing small clubs that we would beat by eight and sometimes 11 goals. Everything that summer was about passing, moving, playing, shooting.

At the age of 32, David changed my role. At Port Vale and Brighton, I had always been a central midfielder in a 4-4-2. I pushed forward, I scored goals. At Luton, I became a holding midfielder, protecting the back four. It cut down on my running and it was a role I came to love. He also made me his captain.

Alan Mullery had asked me to join him at Charlton and there was an offer from Arthur Cox to captain Newcastle but I'd already agreed terms with Luton. As it happened, the first game of the season saw us play Charlton at Kenilworth Road. We beat them, 3-0.

On the Tuesday night, we found ourselves at Queens Park Rangers, who had just had their Astroturf pitch laid at Loftus Road. Luton won, 2-1. That season, Queens Park Rangers would lose only one other match on the Astroturf – against Chelsea on Boxing Day – and they also reached the FA Cup Final. Ours was a heck of a win and we achieved it by playing good passing football.

Their manager, Terry Venables, who wrote a book called *They Used to Play on Grass,* was a big advocate of the new surface and the match programme showed Clive Allen sweeping the pitch. However, Loftus Road in September 1981 bore very little resemblance to the Astroturf pitches you see now. It was rock hard; you ended the game with bruises, grazes and burns.

We won the third game, 2-1, at Bolton to go top of the Second Division but then David decided to change the team for the home fixture against Sheffield Wednesday. He played Raddy Antic as sweeper and we lost, 3-0. We lost the next home game to Cardiff, 3-2, and David, who was one for getting his players together, called a meeting.

David would always start his meetings by turning to one of the younger players, someone like Mitchell Thomas, and asking him what he thought. The idea was that they wouldn't be influenced by the senior pros.

Then he turned to me. I was unsure of myself because Alan Mullery rarely called meetings. At Brighton what he said was usually law.

I said: 'I don't understand why you've changed the team. We have the best side in the division. You've changed it and we've lost twice.' David Pleat took that on board in a way many managers would not. Alan Mullery, I am sure, would not have accepted it.

David changed us back to a 4-3-3. That meeting was in mid-September. The next game saw us play Watford at Kenilworth Road. We won, 4-1. We thrashed Grimsby, 6-0. We lost only two games in the seven months that followed – 3-2 at Newcastle and 4-3 at Barnsley.

We played through midfield. Ricky Hill was on the right. He was one of the best I ever played alongside. He was a man who did my running for me. Ricky played more than 400 games for Luton, won the League Cup with them in 1988 and played for England but I wonder if he shouldn't have gone to a really big club. He was certainly good enough.

In Luton's three-man midfield, a formation that was ahead of its time, Ricky was on the right and to my left was Lil Fuccillo, who had a magical left foot. Lil had been with Luton since he was a schoolboy and had broken his leg playing against Brighton at the Goldstone Ground.

Because of that and because I had come to Kenilworth Road from Brighton, Lil at first would not speak a word to me? Then, I sought him out and said: 'Why are you so frosty with me. It wasn't me who broke your leg.' That broke the ice in our relationship and for the remainder of his stay at Luton – he went to America in 1983 – we were good friends.

Raddy Antic, who died during the writing of this book, was a very talented footballer and was something of a free spirit in that team, although when David Pleat told him what to do, he would do it.

Raddy said David had helped him discover football and how it could be played. However, when Luton changed to a 4-3-3 formation Raddy lost his regular starting place in the side as a sweeper, although his ability remained second to none.

Because we both lived in Harpenden, we would travel together to Luton's training ground at Vauxhall Motors, which was so close to the airport that planes seemed to be flying a few feet above you as we practised our set pieces. He was a man who loved to talk, who loved being around

English players and was always trying to find out more about the game. You could tell he was thinking about going into coaching even then.

He would excel as a manager, taking charge at Real Madrid, Barcelona and Atletico Madrid. He would become the only man in the history of La Liga to manage Spanish football's Big Three. Only one other man, Enrique Fernandez in the 1950s, ever took charge of both Real Madrid and Barcelona. In 1992, midway through the season, he was fired by Real Madrid when they were seven points clear at the top of La Liga. Four years later, he won the league and cup double with Atletico.

Brian Stein led the attack with young Paul Walsh coming through alongside him and to their left would be David Moss. It was probably not a coincidence that Luton's dramatic upswing in fortunes came with David Moss's return from Florida, where he had been playing on loan with Tampa Bay Rowdies.

We won the Second Division title with four games to go and finished eight points clear of Watford, who under Graham Taylor, became our biggest rivals. Their tactics were to play it long and hit the front players, Luther Blissett and Ross Jenkins. David Pleat would never allow us to operate like that.

When we returned to the top flight, Graham Taylor took Watford to second place in the championship behind only Liverpool, while Luton survived only on the last Saturday of the season. I like to think that we were a much better footballing side.

The game that would stick in most of our throats would come the following season, the FA Cup third round in 1984. We were leading 2-0 but with minutes to go Watford were given a free kick and a penalty and scored from both.

The tie went to a replay at Vicarage Road. When John Barnes scored five minutes into the second half, Watford were 3-1 up but Paul Walsh, who was just 21, scored twice to take the match into extra time.

The game was settled by another young striker, Mo Johnston, who had just been signed from Partick Thistle and whose goals would both save Watford from relegation and take them to the FA Cup Final.

Had David, rather than Graham, succeeded Bobby Robson as England manager after the World Cup in Italy, things might have worked out very differently.

I do not mean to disrespect Graham by saying that. Dennis Booth, who was my assistant manager at Hull and played for Graham at Lincoln and Watford, adored the man. However, Graham Taylor and David Pleat had two completely different ways of looking at football.

Tactically, David was ahead of his time. At Tottenham, he was one of the first managers in England to play with a single striker and a five-man midfield. It had been done abroad but England was still wedded to 4-4-2. In 1987 he took Tottenham to third, which was a position they did not better for 30 years. At Luton, he introduced the team to yoga and kick-boxing.

He had built a very good backroom team at Kenilworth Road. David Coates, who had played for Hull City, was his number two. He was an experienced voice, ten years older than the manager.

Trevor Hartley, who ran the reserves, had played for and managed Bournemouth and would go to Tottenham with David Pleat when he took over at White Hart Lane.

That Luton kept performing without David Pleat was due in part to John Moore, who was youth-team coach when I was at the club. John took over as manager and stepped down after only one season, saying he didn't think he was suited to the job. John had, however, led Luton to seventh place in Division One in 1987 which remains the club's highest ever finish. At Kenilworth Road they had beaten Everton, Liverpool, Manchester United and Tottenham.

In my time at Luton, our physio was John Sheridan, who was another that David Pleat rated so highly that he took him to Tottenham. John was on the pitch at Wembley treating Paul Gascoigne when he tore his cruciate ligaments during the 1991 FA Cup final against Nottingham Forest.

Between them the team of Pleat, Coates, Hartley and Moore developed 20 international footballers at Luton, which is an astonishing number when you consider the size of the club.

If Watford had Elton John, Luton had Eric Morecambe. He lived in the same town I did, Harpenden, and owned a beautiful house that overlooked the golf course.

According to his son, Gary, Eric had come to live in Harpenden in 1969 and wanted to support the local football team. Harpenden is roughly halfway between Luton and Watford so they tossed a coin and Luton won. He was so taken with Kenilworth Road that he asked to join the board. He didn't put money into the club and he didn't feel he needed to. The sheer volume of publicity and good PR Eric Morecambe achieved for Luton Town was priceless.

With us, Eric Morecambe was exactly as you might expect, always the comedian. He would come into the dressing room, make us laugh, try to relax us. Out of the corner of your eye, you would see David Pleat, who was trying to be professional, wondering what on earth was going on but Eric's presence seemed to take so much pressure from us.

In Harpenden, he always seemed to be 'on duty'. He would queue up in the butcher's and go into a routine just to make people laugh. When we won promotion in 1982, Luton put up a big marquee on the pitch and he came and danced stupidly with his wife, Joan. He invited us to one of his shows and the degree of professionalism and the attention to the smallest details were astonishing.

Watford may have been the team of the 1982/83 season but Luton made a rapid start back in the First Division. We beat Notts County 5-3 and then put five past Brighton who would end the season reaching the FA Cup Final while being relegated.

In September, we went to Anfield and drew 3-3 with Liverpool while using three goalkeepers – each of whom conceded a goal. Jake Findlay, our regular goalkeeper, was forced off after 38 minutes. These were the days of one substitute, who would almost never be a goalkeeper, so Kirk Stephens moved from right-back to goalkeeper.

Kirk stood no taller than five foot seven and was one of the best attacking right-backs I have ever played with. David Pleat then replaced him with Mal Donaghy. With a quarter of an hour to go, Luton, who have yet to win at Anfield, were leading 3-2, when Craig Johnston, who was Liverpool's substitute, scored the equaliser. Next season we would go back to Anfield, play a specialist goalkeeper throughout and concede six.

I went in goal twice for Port Vale. Both times I was absolutely shaking with nerves. Once was at Swansea, who had a big, bruising centre-forward called Herbie Williams, who had clattered our goalkeeper, Alan Boswell. Almost the first thing I did was to come for a cross and Williams promptly clattered me.

However well Luton started, by April, it seemed likely we would be going down with Brighton. We lost four straight games, culminating in a 5-2 defeat at Watford that left us second bottom. Our problem was inconsistency; it was not until we followed up the Watford defeat by beating Birmingham and Aston Villa that we won two successive matches.

Those victories gave us some breathing space and we followed them up by beating Swansea and taking a point off Southampton and Stoke. On 3 May 1983 Luton were

16th, four places and two points above the relegation zone. Manchester City were third from bottom. We had a game in hand over them and a better goal difference. It would be close but we were confident we would make it.

Our final home game was against Everton. We did slightly better than we had when we played them at Goodison Park in December. Then, we had been thrashed, 5-0. Now, we lost 5-1. To compound everything the teams around us – Manchester City, Birmingham, Coventry and Sunderland – had all won.

That was Saturday afternoon; the Saturday afternoon when we found ourselves in the relegation zone. We still had our game in hand. On the Monday night, we were going to Old Trafford to play Manchester United. David pulled me and said: 'I'll be playing two young lads alongside you – Ray Daniel and Garry Parker.' They were respectively 18 and 17 years old.

'Gaffer, I would never, ever tell you who to play but we are up against Bryan Robson, Remi Moses and Ray Wilkins.' We lost, 3-0.

Luton would go into the last round of matches in the final relegation position, a point behind Manchester City. We would have to go to Maine Road and win.

Meanwhile, David Pleat had agreed for us to play in a testimonial match for Ross Jenkins at Watford that week. I was absolutely dumbstruck that we would be playing a benefit match at the home of our arch rivals a few days before a game that could send us down. I told David I would not be playing. Watford won the match, 4-0.

Luton had played three games in almost as many days and conceded 12 goals. Manchester City only needed a draw at home to ensure their own survival and relegate us. They were entitled to fancy their chances.

Throughout all this, David Pleat remained astonishingly calm. What was more remarkable was that he displayed this calmness while under enormous pressure. He knew that, if Luton were relegated, we might never come back up.

At Brighton I had endured several seasons that were decided on the final day and when I managed Oxford and Port Vale I'd have a couple more. Looking back, everything David Pleat did in that final week was designed to relax us. It was superb man-management.

On the Thursday, he took us to Henlow Grange, a fantastic health spa owned by Stephen Purdew who, amongst others, runs Mottram Hall in Cheshire, a place I have come to know very well since coming to Manchester in 1993. There was no training, just facials, massages and sessions in the steam room. Again, it was something few clubs in 1983 would have done.

On the Friday, we went to Tillington Hall in Staffordshire. He told me: 'You can tell the lads they can have a couple of drinks – no pints, just halves.'

When we got to the dressing room at Maine Road, David made no great speeches. He was never one for that.

His instructions were precise and tactical. We had two advantages. The first was that by playing a weakened team at Old Trafford our midfield was fresher than it might have been. The other was that we knew what we had to do. We had to win.

Manchester City had two choices in front of them. They could take a risk and go for the win or they could try to draw the game. They went for a goalless draw and playing for a draw is one of football's harder tasks.

It was a tight, tense game but with five minutes to go the Manchester City keeper, Alex Williams, punched out a cross that Raddy Antic met on the edge of the area. His shot buried itself in the corner of the City net. Raddy had played in Yugoslavia, Turkey and Spain but he said this was the most important goal he had ever scored.

When the final whistle went, David, dressed in his suit, ran on to the pitch. It was a mixture of a dance, a skip and a run with him waving his hands above his head. It is probably the most played piece of film about Luton Town in their history and David is quite embarrassed whenever he sees it but it demonstrates the amount of pressure we were under.

I was the first person he ran to. He gave me a hug, kissed me and said: 'You can go anywhere you want to.'

I said: 'I know I can, gaffer, my contract's up.' I had signed a two-year deal when I joined Luton and it had been allowed to run out.

The atmosphere at Maine Road was becoming evil. Manchester City had been part of the First Division since 1966. There were more than 40,000 in the ground and some were spilling on to the pitch. As we went down the tunnel, I made to shake Dennis Tueart's hand and he turned around and punched me. I hit him back. Suddenly, everybody seemed to be involved.

Dennis was 32, the same age as me and, like me, was out of contract. He had been told that the only way he would be staying at Manchester City was if they avoided relegation. He said afterwards he was simply overwhelmed by frustration.

When we were back in the dressing room and changed, David Pleat suggested we went upstairs and had a drink with the City players. I said: 'Gaffer, we can't. We've just had a fight with them.'

We decided we would go back to Tillington Hall but as we got on the coach, there were a few Manchester City fans waiting for us. We were told to lie down on the floor of the bus as it pulled away and, as it did, we heard the sound of stones striking the windows.

When we reached Tillington Hall, we met my brother, John, who was chairman of Stafford Rangers. They had also escaped relegation on the same day and had gone there to celebrate. We had the most tremendous party.

The next day, the party continued in Luton. The town felt just as it did in the summer of 1982 when we had won promotion. There was the most incredible atmosphere everywhere you went.

But the parties came to an end as parties always do and I came around to the realisation that I no longer had a contract with the club. I was done at Luton.

Because I was out of contract, the players' union, the PFA, circulated my details across the Football League. I used a telephone answering service to screen any calls that might offer me a job while Denise and I went on holiday.

When we came back, there were messages from Maurice Evans at Reading, from John Bond at Burnley and there was an offer from Bobby Moore to go to Southend, where he was a director, and become a player-coach.

The one that really intrigued me was from Chelsea. They were a division below Luton and in 1983 they had only avoided relegation to the Third Division by two points. However, Chelsea were still a big name and they trained near Heathrow which was commutable from where I was living in Harpenden.

I went to Stamford Bridge to speak to the chairman, Ken Bates, and his manager, John Neal, but we could not agree terms. The following year, Chelsea would be promoted as champions.

Then, I got a phone call from David Pleat.

'What are you doing?'

'I'm speaking to other clubs, gaffer. I'm out of contract.'

'Would you speak to me?'

I went over to Kenilworth Road and talked to David in his car, a big Opel Senator. He told me he would offer me a two-year contract and that, if I wanted to coach or become a manager, he would try to help me out. Naturally, I signed.

Luton started the new season very well. After the Christmas fixtures we were fifth, just two points behind Manchester United in second place. Then came the FA Cup defeat to Watford. It knocked something out of us. After beating Wolves on 21 January, we won only two more games and finished 16th.

Paul Walsh was starting to interest some big clubs. In Luton's first season back in the top flight he was voted Young Player of the Year by the Professional Footballers' Association and then went on tour with England to Australia.

Then, he was a right cocky bastard. I would be forever moaning at him for giving the ball away. Paul had a tendency to shoot or dribble when he would have been better off passing the ball.

In the summer of 1984, he was transferred to Liverpool and I think he learnt to pass at Anfield. People like Kenny Dalglish would not tolerate selfishness in a footballer. They would demand the ball.

When, towards the end of his career, I signed him for Manchester City, Paul was a totally different player. At Liverpool and then at Tottenham, he had become a complete footballer.

Paul Walsh wasn't the only one to be leaving Luton in the summer of 1984. It was the summer when I had the chance to fulfil a boyhood dream.

Wolverhampton Wanderers had always been my team and at the age of 35 it looked like I would finally be pulling on the old gold shirt. Wolves had just been relegated from the First Division, Tommy Docherty had been appointed as manager and I was being offered the role of player-coach. I could go back to Cannock where I had grown up and play at Molineux.

I didn't make the move. Hull City were looking for a new manager and I thought I could be my own man in Yorkshire. Had I gone to Wolves I would have been part of the most disastrous spell in their history when in successive seasons they were relegated from the First to the Fourth Division. The Doc was sacked after one season in charge and, in all probability, I would have been fired with him.

Hull were an intriguing proposition. On the final day of the season, they had gone to Turf Moor needing to beat Burnley by three clear goals to win promotion to the Second Division ahead of Sheffield United on goal difference.

Brian Marwood scored twice but the elusive third goal never came and Hull missed out on promotion by a single goal. Hull's manager was Colin Appleton, who had come within an ace of winning the club back-to-back promotions.

However, Appleton resigned to manage Swansea, who in two seasons had collapsed from the First to the Third

Division. He lasted only a few months in Wales and by 1986 Swansea had completed their slide to the Fourth Division.

Hull's chairman, Don Robinson, told me Jack Charlton, Emlyn Hughes, Malcolm Allison and David Pleat had all recommended me for the job. As endorsements go, they didn't come much better than that.

I met Don at the Queens Hotel in Leeds. My younger brother, Alan, lived in Leeds so I asked him plenty of questions about the state of football in Yorkshire and drove up for a 9am meeting.

It was a long way to come for five minutes and a cup of coffee. There were no conversations about tactics or how I saw the job going. Don came straight to the point. He wanted me to become Hull's player-manager and gave me a piece of paper with a proposed salary.

'Is that for playing or managing?'

'Both.'

'I'm terribly sorry but that's half what I'm on just playing for Luton and I can stay. I've got another year on my contract.'

'If you do well, I'll look after you. The job's yours. Ring me in 24 hours.'

I knew deep inside that it was a matter of time before I had to drop down a division if I wanted to carry on playing. Luton were in the top flight and they would stay there until 1992. It was becoming ever harder for me at 35 to keep up with the pace of it all. You would be facing Liverpool with

Graeme Souness and Ian Rush or Everton with Peter Reid and Andy Gray, the next week would see you trying to stop Glenn Hoddle or Bryan Robson. It was a tough level.

The question I asked myself was whether I stayed on at Luton and became a bit-part player – which is something I had never been – or went into a job that might secure my future in the game. I rang Denise, to see how she felt about moving from Harpenden. The reality is that Hull is a long way from anywhere. She was happy to take the family north. I spoke to David Pleat, who told me I should back myself and take the job. I rang Don Robinson. I was now a manager.

David Moss (Luton Town 1978–1985)

In 1981 I had just finished playing in America for Tampa Bay Rowdies and was waiting to come home to Luton when David Pleat phoned and said: 'I've signed a new captain.'

'Who is it?'

'It's Brian Horton.'

'Bloody hell, no. He hates me.'

I had first encountered Brian when I was playing for Swindon and he was at Brighton. He would give me the most tremendous stick before trying to kick me from one end of the field to the other. He was a ferocious competitor.

On New Year's Day 1977, we played Brighton and were 4-0 up when the referee abandoned the game because the pitch was waterlogged and had become unplayable. Needless to say, Brian was the most vociferous of the Brighton players that the game could not continue 'because somebody will get seriously injured'.

We ended up becoming great mates at Luton and roomed together. It still didn't stop him being on my case for 90 minutes of every match. I used to say to him during games: 'Get off my bloody back.' He was a good captain because he was so demanding.

David Pleat was very shrewd in the way he put that Luton team together. I was a Third Division player at Swindon and David took a chance on me. It was a team assembled, relatively speaking, for peanuts but we all felt we had something to prove.

I didn't play in the relegation decider at Manchester City. Our last home game had been a 5-1 thrashing by Everton. I had scored the opening goal and then done my rib cartilage. The pressure on us was unbelievable. There were three or four of us in the stands at Maine Road and you could not bear to watch the game. Afterwards, as we were trying to get out of Moss Side, the police got on the bus and said: 'Everybody on the floor.' Then the stones started hitting the side of the bus.

Tiger

(Games 573–766)

DON Robinson had been many things. He had been a professional wrestler who became a wrestling promoter and went on to run charter flights to Las Vegas.

Don seemed to be connected with almost everything in Scarborough. He owned the Opera House, the Grand Hotel, he was president of the Scarborough cricket festival and owned the town's football team, which under Neil Warnock won promotion to the Football League in 1987.

Five years before, he had bought a majority stake in Hull City for £250,000. They'd won promotion from Division Four in his first season at Boothferry Park and missed out on a place in Division Two on goal difference in his second. For a man who claimed to know nothing about football it wasn't a bad start.

You could tell Don's style by the fact that I joined up with the team in Florida, which was an unusual place for a Third Division club to go on a summer tour in 1984. We would be playing Tampa Bay Rowdies, managed by Rodney Marsh and coached by Malcolm Allison, who I learned had recommended me for the manager's job at Hull.

When we put on our kit, we realised how this trip had been paid for. The shirts had 'Arrow Air' emblazoned on them. Arrow Air were an airline based in Miami and they had given us free flights in exchange for a shirt sponsorship deal.

Being a player-manager was tough. As assistant manager, I inherited Chris Chilton, who had been Hull City's record goalscorer. I also had Dennis Booth who had been at Hull for the past four years. He was the same age as me, played in a similar position and also did some coaching. He became one of my best mates in football.

Tom Wilson was the club's youth-team coach. Tom had played for Hull as a central defender in the 1960s and then joined a firm of solicitors. He came back to Boothferry Park in 1986 and would have three spells as caretaker manager. His grandson, Harry Cardwell, joined Grimsby as a centre-forward.

Jeff Radcliffe, our physio, completed the team. He had been at the club long before I joined and had even played for Hull on a pre-season tour of Holland in 1979 because they had so many injuries. They not only played the physio, they asked the coach driver to put some boots on. In April 1988, a few days after I'd left the club, Tottenham sent up a team to Boothferry Park for his testimonial.

Three of my first four games as manager were against Lincoln City. We played them at Sincil Bank on the opening day of the season.

Lincoln were managed by Colin Murphy and had a good side with players like John Fashanu, Mick Harford and Steve Thompson.

We drew nil-nil and on the Tuesday we were back again in the first leg of the League Cup. I'd tweaked my thigh in a pre-season game at North Ferriby and it hadn't improved in the league game at Lincoln. I left myself out and played Dennis in my position.

We won 1-0 and on the Saturday we had Bournemouth, managed by Harry Redknapp, at Boothferry Park. Dennis told me that I couldn't leave him out now and I told him that was exactly what I was doing. I played a lad called Mike Ring, a winger I'd bought in from Brighton, went 4-2-4 in my first home game and Hull won, 3-0.

One of the biggest problems of being a player-manager is how do you instil discipline when you're one of the players at fault? In November, we were playing Leyton Orient. They were managed by Frank Clark and at half-time we were 3-1 down. Orient had absolutely murdered us. I knew I was playing badly.

As we went into the dressing rooms at Brisbane Road, I turned to Chris and said: 'This is going to be hard but I want you to get stuck into us – including me. Get some verbals going.' Chris duly tore into us.

Hull won the game, 5-4, although with half an hour left, we were 4-1 down. Steve Massey made it 4-2 from a Billy Whitehurst cross. I put a header against the bar, which I thought had gone over the line, and Andy Flounders bundled it in. I would never come closer to scoring a goal for Hull.

It was now 4-3 and you could sense something remarkable was happening. Stan McEwan put away a penalty, given for handball, to level the scores and, when Andy Flounders put away his second, we had scored four times in 23 minutes.

I inherited a good side. Steve McClaren was in midfield, Peter Skipper was at centre-half and our attack was led by Billy Whitehurst, a big, ferociously tough Yorkshireman.

Billy liked a drink – he wound up running a pub on Bramall Lane – and he could be hard to handle. However, we got him fitter and played him in a system that suited him – with wingers that put in crosses for him.

He was very hard, very physical and trained the way he played. He never pulled out of anything. I wouldn't have liked to have been up against him. Because I was no longer captain at Hull, I used to be among the last to come out and I can remember hearing this roar behind me as I went out at Booth-ferry. I turned around and it was Billy, roaring at the opposition.

He was 24, he knew scouts were watching him and there were reports he was wanted by Sheffield Wednesday. He would come and see me about them and I told him: 'Billy, if it's right for you and it's right for the club and the money's right, we will sell you. But it will be my decision alone.'

In the summer of 1985, I had a call from Willie McFaul who had just become manager of Newcastle. He offered me £230,000 for Billy. I rang Don Robinson and recommended we do the transfer.

Don replied: 'I know Lord Westwood, the chairman of Newcastle. I think I could do a better deal.'

I said: 'Don, don't screw the deal. It's a good deal for us and it's a good deal for Billy. He deserves to go to a club like Newcastle. For God's sake don't mess it up.'

He rang me back later that day and announced: 'I told you I'd get you more money.'

'What did you get from Newcastle?'

'£232,000.'

'Fucking well done. You've put the whole transfer at risk for £2,000.'

Billy scored 24 times in Hull's promotion to the Second Division and one goal I will always remember came against Derby, who were managed by Arthur Cox, who had given me a free transfer from Walsall and who would keep cropping up in my story.

We played them at Boothferry Park in March. It was 2-2. Billy Askew, who went to Newcastle a few years after Whitehurst, would take corners from the left-hand side with a wonderful technique.

With time almost up, he drilled in a ball and Whitehurst came in at the back post and scored one of the best headers I have ever seen.

For a few months we paired Billy with Frankie Bunn, who I had played with at Luton. Embarrassingly, given the fact David Pleat had been my mentor for three years, we found ourselves at a tribunal arguing over his fee.

The tribunal found in our favour and, as we walked out, David congratulated me before turning to my chairman and asking if Luton could have the fee in a single payment. Don agreed so we both got something out of it.

Frankie only played with Billy for a few months but after Whitehurst's departure he proved a highly effective striker scoring 23 goals in 95 league games for Hull. However, in 1987 he ran into some difficulties in his personal life which meant we had to sell him to Oldham, where he will always be remembered for scoring six times in a League Cup tie against Scarborough.

Peter Skipper's goal at Fellows Park meant we won promotion at Walsall with two games to go. For some reason I didn't play that game but Don Robinson came over and said: 'Jump on my back and I'll carry you round the fans.'

I told the chairman that I wouldn't be doing that but later Don saw my parents in the directors' room, pulled out some notes from his pocket, handed them to my dad and said: 'Please take Mrs Horton out for dinner.'

He was generous like that. Our last home game of the season was at home to York and Don stood on the terraces handing out champagne to the fans. He looked after the players. The team went away every summer – to Marbella, to Estepona, we went to Gibraltar, where he had a casino.

Even though we had gone up and Derby had finished no higher than seventh, Steve McClaren, who was an excellent midfielder, chose go to the Baseball Ground under freedom of contract. Derby went up the following season.

I had won promotion in my first full seasons at Brighton, Luton and now Hull and, after we'd gone up in 1985, Don asked if I would become a director of the club. I played for the club, I managed it and now I was on the board.

They set up pictures of me with a briefcase and an umbrella. Don told me I was to run the club for him because he would be spending most of his time in Scarborough.

One of the first things I had to vote on as a director was Don Robinson's proposal to lease out Hull's gym to the city's cricket club.

Don was always looking for ways to raise money and we had a beautiful gym behind one of the stands. I told him that, if it was hired out for winter nets twice a week, where were his footballers going to go on a Tuesday and Thursday night? I voted against him, which he neither liked nor expected.

Although Don Robinson was reluctant to interfere in team affairs, he did like to hang out with the players and he gave them a room under one of the stands at Boothferry Park which they could turn into a bar. He arranged a deal with the brewery in Hull to supply it with beer and lager.

Once, we lost at home and I decided to close the bar before the players could come in. Don went into the dressing room and asked: 'Why have you closed the bar?'

'Because we have just lost. I am not allowing them to drink after a game which we have just lost in front of our own fans.'

He accepted that, which for the kind of man he was, a self-made millionaire, was unusual. Don Robinson was never a man who believed he was always right.

Usually, I would travel up to Scarborough to meet him for lunch and talk over club affairs. After we had won promotion to the Second Division, the players asked for improved bonuses. Because I was still a player and I would be one of the beneficiaries, this put me in an awkward situation so I asked Don to rule on it.

Don refused the request for bigger win bonuses, although I did persuade him to meet the players and explain the situation. I went into my office while he met them in the dressing rooms and after two minutes he came back out.

'I've sorted it,' he said. 'I've given it to them.'

'So, you have told me to tell them that they can't have the payments and within two minutes you've told them to their faces that they can. Now, I look the bad guy and, suddenly, you're the good guy.' He just started laughing.

Hull were back in the Second Division for the first time since 1978. Boothferry Park had a magnificent pitch. It had a huge terrace behind one goal and a cut-off one behind the other because that end of the ground had been sold to a supermarket.

When I went to Humberside in 1984, the two rugby league teams, Hull and Hull Kingston Rovers, were two of the biggest clubs in the country. We started to overtake them in terms of gates and for some big matches we would attract around 18,000 to Boothferry.

Hull had a very good youth policy, inspired by two teachers, Dave King and Freddie Cowell, who had a great gift of spotting young players.

They were instrumental in our signing Andy Payton, who had been released by Burnley as a 15-year-old. He was sold to Middlesbrough for £700,000. Leigh Jenkinson, who was a very quick winger, was another they discovered. He was sold to Coventry for £250,000.

The jewel was Nicky Barmby, whose dad, Jeff, had played for Scarborough in four FA Trophy finals. Nicky was ten when I became Hull manager but he was such an obvious talent that we couldn't keep him and he went to the FA's school of excellence and signed for Tottenham when he was 16.

Hull was a big city with a big catchment area which had rarely been tapped for talent. We set up an academy to find good young players and Nicky's dad, Jeff, was one of the coaches.

We didn't want to join the FA's academy system but we were made to because the FA threatened us that, if Hull continued to go it alone, they would give other clubs in Yorkshire permission to set up satellite academies in our area.

We were building a good side. I bought Richard Jobson from Watford, who were in the First Division under Graham Taylor, for £40,000. I bought Garry Parker, who'd made his debut at 17 against Manchester United, from David Pleat and bought another Luton player, Frankie Bunn.

In 1986, Hull finished sixth in the Second Division, which was the third-highest position in the club's history. In 1910, they were third and missed out on promotion to the top flight on goal difference. In 1971, they had finished fifth. Sixth was a real achievement for a newly promoted side but the play-offs were introduced the following season and, had they been in place then, we would have qualified for them.

I should have celebrated by buying Mark Bright to lead Hull's attack. He was playing at Leicester but had struggled to establish himself at Filbert Street. I had gone to watch Bright at a reserve game where it was clear he was a class apart from the rest.

Usually a manager or a scout watching a player will leave ten minutes before the end to avoid the traffic but I decided to stay and talk to the Leicester manager, Bryan Hamilton, who offered me Bright for £45,000. I took the offer back to Don Robinson, who accepted it.

I then met Mark to discuss personal terms. When he had moved from Port Vale to Leicester for £33,000 two years before he had been paid a £10,000 signing-on fee and naturally expected something similar from Hull. Don Robinson absolutely refused to pay it. Mark went to Crystal Palace, where he formed the Wright and Bright strike partnership and in 1992 he was sold to Sheffield Wednesday for £1.3m.

My final game as a professional footballer came against Crystal Palace. I was marking someone; we went up for a high ball. Bang! There was an elbow in my face, my eye was split open and, with blood spurting down my shirt, I ran over to the referee to ask how on earth he had missed that.

The physio came on and told me I had to go off for treatment. 'I'm staying on. I'm not finished here,' I said, and went off in a rage. Soon afterwards, I did something stupid, launched myself into a reckless tackle and got myself sent off trying to do someone.

After the match, the chairman came into my office and said: 'I rather liked that.'

'Well, I didn't. It's absolutely stupid. I am fining myself, as I would fine any other player, and I am retiring tonight.'

I then found the referee and told him that because he had failed to spot something so blatant I had lost control and was packing it in. I still turned out for the reserves but as a front-line footballer that was me done.

One of the hardest things I had to do came on New Year's Day 1987. We were playing a Yorkshire derby against Barnsley in an early kick-off. As we arrived at the ground, Richard Chetham, one of the directors, came over to me and said: 'I need to tell you that I went to a party last night and Stan McEwan was there.'

Stan was a good lad, a defender from Wishaw in Scotland and I decided to play him and then confront him about the story after the match. We lost 4-3 to Barnsley and Stan had been at fault for one of the goals.

I came into the dressing room after the match and asked the players to sit down and said: 'Stan, were you at a party last night? Don't lie to me because I know you were there.'

He said: 'Yes I was.'

'Get your boots and leave the dressing room. You will never play for me again.'

The players around me were saying: 'Come on gaffer, that's harsh.'

'He has cost us the game and it's a Yorkshire derby. You know the rules, I know the rules – you don't go to a party the night before a game.'

The Professional Footballers' Association got in touch with me and told me I could not take this kind of action against Stan McEwan. I was surprised by this because I had been a PFA rep at every club I'd worked at.

The PFA told me I could not simply sack him. McEwan had to play a certain number of games. In that case, I told them, I would play him in the reserves and take him off at half-time in each match. If he wanted to train, he could come in the afternoons when we were finished. The situation resolved itself when Stan was transferred to Wigan.

In 2007, I went back to Hull as assistant manager to Phil Brown. The place had changed completely. Boothferry Park had gone and the club was now in a brand-new stadium, where some of the former players were working in the lounges, entertaining corporate clients.

I told Phil that we should get them together at a pub in North Ferriby, a village which has great views across to the Humber Bridge and which was where I'd lived when I was manager. The old players would have stories and insights about the club and Phil would not have met them before.

One of the players working the lounges was Stan McEwan and, as I went to Ferriby, I though this might be quite an awkward night. Stan was one of the first to come in. He went to the bar and said to me: 'Is it okay if I have a beer now, gaffer?' It broke the ice.

Hull did not play at Wembley until 2008 but 22 years before the play-off final, we came within one game of the Twin Towers.

The deaths at Heysel before the 1985 European Cup Final had been met with a blanket ban of English clubs from Europe. The Football League responded by creating two competitions. The Super Cup, which was for the six clubs that would have qualified for European competitions but for the ban – Everton, Manchester United, Norwich, Liverpool, Tottenham and Southampton.

The rest of the top two divisions played for the Full Members Cup, which unlike the Super Cup, had a Wembley final. We were drawn against Manchester City in the northern final which was played home and away.

My school team, St Chads, which I captained to a league and cup double.

Combining building site work and playing for Hednesford was one of the most enjoyable times of my life.

Scoring for Hednesford at Cross Keys.

▲ **Above: The Staffs Senior Cup side of 1969/70, featuring Brian Horton, circled**

Winning the 1970 Staffordshire Senior Cup, my last game for Hednesford.

Horton double mauls the Lions

Division Three
Port Vale 2, Millwall 0

PORT VALE kept the entertainment stakes high with another confident performance to see off a robust Millwall side.

Having scored four goals in their last match, Vale were not about to take their foot of the pedal and came out strongly, with Brian Horton and Terry Bailey commanding the midfield. But the finishing touches were still lacking, with Derek Brownbill guilty of wasting a good chance.

Millwall did not show any signs as an attacking force until the 20th minute, but Saul could only fire a hopeful shot well over the bar and Salvage saw his volley go harmlessly wide.

Vale kept their composure while some heavy tackles went in and finally got their rewards when Horton volleyed in Mick Cullerton's corner for his first goal of the season.

The second half saw no halt to the Vale charge as they continued to pin Millwall back in their own half, with Horton running the show.

It was Horton who made the game safe just after the hour as he combined again with Cullerton to glance home a header to cap off an impressive display. Millwall finally started to test the Vale defence and keeper John Connaughton saved well from Davies, while Terry Lees cleared off the line from Saul.

Horton almost sealed the win, and his hat-trick, in the last minute as he intercepted a Millwall throw and let fly with a cracking shot that just missed the post.

PORT VALE: Connaughton, Tartt, Griffiths, Ridley, Harris, Horton, McLaren, Lees, Cullerton, Bailey, Brownbill. Sub: Williams.
MILLWALL: Goddard, Evans, Jones, Dorney, Kitchener, Walker, Lee, Brisley, Davies, Saul, Salvage. Sub: Welsh.

HEAD OF THE PACK: Brian Horton scored twice for Port Vale, the second goal coming from a header.

I was a much more attacking player at Port Vale. Scoring against Millwall, November 1975.

Port Vale, my first professional club. The gifted Tommy McLaren is sitting behind me.

A pre-season portrait as captain of Port Vale.

Vale hard man Horton signs for Albion

PETER TAYLOR WATCHES BRIAN HORTON SIGN

Signing for Peter Taylor at Brighton. March 1976.

Attacking for Brighton at the Goldstone Ground.

Waving to the crowd as Brighton just miss out on promotion in April 1978. Harry Bloom, Tony Bloom's grandfather, looks on behind Peter Ward.

Attacking against Bristol Rovers. April 1979.

Teddy Maybank stands between me and Mark Lawrenson. The reason for all the guns is we are about to play Arsenal.

There was no finer feeling than celebrating at the Goldstone.

Leading out Brighton for the first game in the top flight. August 1979.

Shielding the ball from Liam Brady. It only worked for so long. We lost, 4-0.

Looking for a way through against Aston Villa.

With Peter Ward and Alan Mullery at Hove Park. Astonishingly for a top-flight club, Brighton did not possess their own training ground.

Celebrating promotion with Luton, April 1982.

On the cover with David Pleat and on the road to a thousand games with Hull.

In manager's office. 1984.

Lifting the Second Division championship trophy at Kenilworth Road, 1982

MIRROR SPORT | Always leading the fie

GOLDEN NUGGET

Boss Brian a Hull of a fella ..

THERE'S a golden glow about boom-again Hull City that doesn't stop at the colour of their amber shirts . . .

By TED MACAULEY

Hunger

Lighten

'I've a team that wants to get on with it'

I was soon making headlines. Hull won promotion in my first season at Boothferry Park.

The reason I am photographed holding a briefcase is that I've been asked to join the board at Hull City.

EXPRESS SOCCER — Hull's top flight team

Just the job

Horton salutes old pals' act

By John Donoghue

BRIAN HORTON yesterday thanked the pal who has helped him re-introduce Hull City to the Second Division top flight.

Unbeaten

Lighten

HORTON ... 'I'm in a deadly serious business'

EXPRESS SPORT ... ALWAYS ON THE BALL FOR SOCCER ... THE PAPER THAT CARES ABOUT YOUR CLUB

With Mark Lawrenson at Oxford in 1988. In front of us are the backroom staff at the Manor Ground. Coach, David Moss, general manager, Maurice Evans, physio, John Clinkard and coach, David Fogg.

Manchester City manager, August 1993.

With perhaps my best signing, Uwe Rösler. March 1994.

Celebrating after a 3-2 win at soon-to-be champions, Blackburn. April 1995.

HEARTENED HORTON PROVES THERE IS LIFE AFTER CITY

Brian's reborn

BRIAN HORTON leans forward across his manager's desk beneath the main stand at Huddersfield Town's futuristic McAlpine Stadium.

He looks relaxed and younger than when he was sacked by Francis Lee as manager of Manchester City two summers ago.

Perhaps the security of working for a board at Huddersfield which has faith him has helped to shed the years — or maybe it's just that he's shaved off his beard since leaving Maine Road.

Whatever, he ponders the question carefully: "Am I bitter about the way I was treated by Francis Lee?" he repeats.

"Not in the slightest. I enjoyed every minute of my time at Maine Road ... well, ALMOST every minute.

"Put it this way, I have never once regretted my decision to accept the City manager's job when it was offered to me.

"It was my burning ambition to manage a major Premiership club and Manchester City gave me that opportunity.

"That is something which no-one can ever take away from me. In fact it is the proudest item on my CV.

"And I believe the experience I gained at managing at the highest level at Maine Road helped me considerably in landing the job here at Huddersfield Town.

"So far from being bitter about my time as City's manager, I have a lot to thank them for."

 By **PAUL HINCE** •••• CHIEF SPORTS WRITER

However, beneath that layer of genuine gratitude for his time spent with the Blues, you get the impression talking to this proud and dignified Midlander that he was wounded deeply when he was told by Lee shortly after the end of season 1994-95 that his services were no longer required.

Politely, but firmly, he refuses to discuss his relationship with chairman Lee during their time together at Maine Road.

Push him on that point and you are met with the famous Horton stare which can freeze water at 20 paces.

But he does admit to wondering in his quieter moments where the Blues would be today had chairman Lee demonstrated a touch more patience and a little more trust.

"Of course I think about it," he concedes. "City were relegated after I left and I felt genuine regret for the players and all the friends I made during my time at Maine Road.

"And then came all the highly-publicised failures when they were attempting to find a replacement for Alan Ball.

"You cannot help thinking that if they had left well alone in the first place, they would never have had those problems to sort out.

"But you cannot dwell on what might have been.

"I was fortunate to be appointed as manager of a very ambitious club in Huddersfield Town and all my energies are now devoted to bringing some success back to this club."

Horton and his Yorkshire terriers will be bidding for three promotion points when they travel across the Pennines tomorrow for the Roses clash against Oldham Athletic at Boundary Park.

"Oldham gave me my first lesson about the strength of the First Division," Horton recalls.

"My very first match as manager at Huddersfield was against Oldham and they beat us 3-0, although to this day I believe that they were flattered by the scoreline.

"Graeme Sharp has had a very tough introduction to soccer management after taking over from Joe Royle at Boundary Park.

"Oldham had a very poor start to the season and he must have felt the pressure which all us managers are subjected to when their team are struggling at the wrong end of a League table.

"But I always had a feeling that Oldham were a better team than their League position indicated.

"The Oldham chairman Ian Stott must take some of the credit for the team's improved results.

"It would have been easy for him to have given in to the demands of some of his club's supporters earlier in the season and to have shown Graeme the exit door.

"But the chairman stood by his manager and bit by bit Oldham are starting to turn the corner. Perhaps there is a lesson in there, somewhere."

■ ON SONG ... Brian Horton

Huddersfield had not been part of the top flight since 1972 but after a rapid start to my first season we could start to dream.

Managing a Football League XI at Huddersfield against a Serie B XI. Steve McClaren is alongside me.

The Huddersfield squad awaits the start of the 1997/98 season.

Trying out Huddersfield's new kit in the summer of 1997. Assistant manager, Dennis Booth, is alongside me.

I CAN'T WAIT

Pictures: Jim Holden

34747-B12

Horton relishes big challenge

NEW Albion boss Brian Horton is relishing one of the most difficult jobs in football.

He cannot wait to get stuck into it after "the worst period of my life" since Huddersfield sacked him in October.

Horton, 49, is the Seagulls' fifth manager in just over four years. They have no home, very little money and are the next-worst team in the country.

He admits: "It's one of the most difficult jobs. We are second-bottom of the bottom division, so that goes without saying, but that's a challenge I relish.

"I never had money at my other clubs, Hull, Oxford and even Manchester City, but that's not a problem. It's a challenge and a huge challenge."

Horton's had plenty of time to work on improving his golf handicap over the past four months. He has been keeping himself busy with media work and watching games, but that's no substitute for the day-to-day involvement he had enjoyed for 34 years until Huddersfield swung the axe.

Nightmare

"I'm a football person and I missed working, that's the bottom line," he said. "It's the first time I have been out of the game since I was 15. It's a nightmare when Saturday comes and you put Teletext on.

"I picked and chose games, because I didn't want to look like a leech sitting in the stands waiting for a manager to get the sack.

"I've done TV work for Channel Five and Sky and radio work in Manchester, but it's been a nightmare being out of it, the worst period of my life."

The nightmare ended for 'Nobby' yesterday morning when he agreed to a temporary contract for the rest of the season. Now he is ready to throw himself into

by Andy Naylor

the task at hand with the all-consuming passion he showed throughout his playing career.

"It's going to be night and day for 12 games and 18 weeks," he said. "There is lots to assess. I know the northern scene more than the south, because I've been up there longer. I need to get round as many games as I can."

Horton played 252 of those, the majority as captain, for Albion during the Seagulls' glorious rise from the old Third Division to the First. Returning to the club as manager is almost, but not quite, his dream job.

"I've always had it in the back of my mind that one day I would love to manage the club, but I would have liked it to have been in better circumstances.

"It was always my number one dream to walk back into Alan Mullery's office as manager at the Goldstone.

"It's been close a couple of times, but it never quite materialised."

Horton added: "I don't want to harp on about the old days. They have gone, but for my last game we had 26,000 against Leeds United. That shows what can be done."

LENDING AN EAR: Brian Horton listens to Albion chairman Dick Knight

In February 1998 I returned to manage Brighton, a club unrecognisable from the one I had left 17 years before.

We beat City, 2-1, at Boothferry Park and it was 1-0 to City at Maine Road going into the last minute when Jim Melrose, who had joined Manchester City from Celtic, scored the winner. With the goal went my last chance of playing at Wembley. Manchester City lost 5-4 to Chelsea in one the most remarkable finals the old stadium had ever staged.

I had largely stopped playing after our first season in the Second Division. Towards the end, I played myself as a sweeper in front of the back four. Dennis Booth was by now the assistant manager because I had moved Chris Chilton to take charge of the youth team.

Dennis was a good assistant in that he could laugh and joke with the players and be quite serious with me. In my last days as a player he nicknamed me Jacques Cousteau because I was going so deep and, to make the point, he bought me a pair of flippers.

Looking back, we were ahead of our time at Hull. The sweeper system became fashionable during the 1990 World Cup. Despite accusations from the media on Humberside that Hull were becoming 'a defensive team' we beat Millwall 3-0 and Carlisle 4-0 in our first two games using the system.

Dennis Booth had come to Hull in 1980 after seven years with Graham Taylor at Lincoln and Watford. In 1987 Graham phoned me. He had left Watford to take charge of Aston Villa, who had just been relegated to the Second Division, and wanted to take Dennis with him as a coach.

When I rang the chairman to tell him there had been an approach from Aston Villa for Dennis, Don Robinson's first reaction was: 'Don't tell him.'

I told Don that Dennis was my best pal in football. If I didn't tell him there was an offer to work at Villa Park and he subsequently bumped into Graham Taylor, what would that do for our friendship?

When I called Dennis in, he said he didn't want the job at Aston Villa and he was happy at Hull. I told him he had to speak to Graham Taylor because Aston Villa was a much bigger club than Hull City. It was a golden opportunity.

He went to Birmingham to speak to Graham and when he came back he told me he had turned the job down. When I asked why he explained he had once applied for a job at Watford as the youth-team coach and he hadn't got it. 'That's always stood in my mind,' he said. 'Now it's 1-1. He turned me down, now I've turned him down.'

I told the chairman that, as he had shown loyalty to Hull by turning down Aston Villa, the club should give Dennis a new contract which should include a company car. I was the only one on the management side who had one – a lovely Ford Granada.

One of our directors was also a director of the Ford garage, Crystal Motors. We thought we would get a beaten-up old car and present it to him as a joke.

We found this old Ford Zephyr with bench seats and a column chain and drove it round to the supermarket car park by the ground. We called Dennis over, thanked him for sticking with us and presented him with this old car as a show of thanks.

The joke fell flat because Dennis had no interest in cars or clothes or anything except football. Without any trace of irony, he said: 'That's nice.' He took it for a drive and when the chairman asked what he thought Dennis told him it drove very well. Eventually, we had to tell him that this wasn't his company car and there was a Ford Sierra waiting for him.

Towards the end of my time at Hull, I made a fundamental mistake. I had a call from Ronnie Fenton, who was assistant to Brian Clough at Nottingham Forest, saying they were interested in Garry Parker. They were prepared to offer £270,000.

I told Ronnie I would be interested in a young full-back they had at the City Ground called Brett Williams. He replied that Forest would do a deal for £200,000 plus Williams.

I should have kept Garry Parker, who was a very good midfielder, at least until the end of the season but I was caught up with the idea of making a big profit for the club.

We had bought Parker from Luton for £72,000 so Hull would be making more than three times his original price. We had money in the bank, we were assured of a comfortable mid-table finish. I told the chairman we could spend £1m in the summer – the biggest spend the club had ever had. Don Robinson thought it a fantastic idea.

Garry had collar-length hair and Ronnie Fenton had told me to make sure he had it cut before he met Brian Clough. 'If Brian sees him with that hair, he won't sign him.'

Without telling him the name of the club, I told Garry that Hull had received an offer for him and I would drive him down to meet them the next day but that he should get his hair cut otherwise the deal would be off.

When I picked him up, Garry had had the smallest of trims but, fortunately when we arrived at the City Ground, Brian Clough wasn't there. Ronnie Fenton took Garry into his office and I went to speak to Brett Williams, who had just turned 20.

As soon as I told Brett about the deal to take him to Hull he burst into tears and said he didn't want to leave Nottingham Forest. As soon as Ronnie had finished discussing terms with Garry Parker, I told him the kid was so upset I couldn't possibly insist on the transfer. 'I know,' said Ronnie. 'They never want to leave Forest because they get looked after here.'

We went back to the original deal, £270,000 in cash. Brett Williams justified his desire to stay by appearing for Nottingham Forest in the 1992 League Cup Final against Manchester United.

Garry Parker played in four Wembley finals for Forest and won the League Cup in 1997 with Leicester. It was a great move for him but, had he stayed at Hull for another couple of months, our season might have ended better and I might have stayed at Boothferry Park.

There is always a time as a manager when you can feel things shifting beneath your feet without quite knowing why. I said to Dennis: 'There's something not right with the chairman. Do you think our relationship with him is okay?'

'What are you talking about?' Dennis replied. 'You're like his son.'

It had been a strange season. Hull did not lose a league game at Boothferry Park until the end of February when we went down 2-1 to Sheffield United. Equally, we'd not won a game since beating Leeds in January.

We were playing Swindon on the Tuesday night. We'd been a long time without a win but we were not in any danger of going down and I thought I'd use the game to try out a few of the younger players with a view to next season.

At half time we were one up but Swindon under Lou Macari were a big, strong team and after the interval they battered us to win 4-1.

I was aware of a few rumblings from the crowd as the final whistle went but nothing that should have had me panicking. As I came off the pitch, Don Robinson was waiting for me.

'I need to speak to you.'

We went into my office and Don said: 'Something's got to give, Brian. It can't go on like this.'

Suddenly, I knew what was coming. 'Just say what you've got to say, Don.'

'Well, I'm sacking you.'

He expected me to blow up because I could be very volatile in those days but I just replied: 'Okay.'

'What do you mean it's okay?'

'Don, we have had some wonderful times together but you're right, it's time to go. Do you want to tell the players or shall I?'

'I'll do it.'

I used the time to tell Dennis Booth, I told my wife, Denise, who was upstairs and I phoned my parents because I did not want the first they knew about it to be from the papers.

Don then came back into my office, looking upset. 'The players have just absolutely crucified me in the dressing room.'

'Well, I thought they would, Don. We have a good team and they didn't see it coming.'

'Would you consider staying on?'

'Are you kidding? You've just told the players you have sacked me. It's finished, Don. What are we going to do if we lose again at the weekend? Are you going to sack me again?'

I saw him the next morning at Boothferry Park, and he made me an offer to settle my contract. I didn't realise I had to resign as a director before he could formally sack me as the club's manager.

The settlement was much less than I was expecting. I told the chairman I'd raised £1m in player sales for the club and I thought my contract should be paid up properly.

Hull would make profits after I'd left. Richard Jobson, bought from Watford for £40,000, went to Oldham for

£460,000. Tony Norman, who was a fine goalkeeper, was sold to Sunderland for £500,000 in the summer of 1988. Alex Dyer, a defensive midfielder, who we'd bought from Blackpool for £27,000, was sold to Crystal Palace for ten times that fee.

After my protest, Don Robinson gave me a cheque there and then. Two days later he sent flowers to my wife and then asked if we could meet for lunch to discuss coming back to Hull. I told him that was a non-starter.

I came back to Boothferry Park when I was manager of Oxford. It was an absolutely foul Tuesday night in April 1989. Billy Whitehurst was back at Hull; the rain was slicing down and the wind was howling off the North Sea. I wouldn't let the team warm up on the pitch; we just did the exercises in the dressing room.

Oxford won the game, 2-1.

Eddie Gray had succeeded me as manager but he went at the end of the season and Don Robinson brought back Colin Appleton, who'd been his first manager when he took control of Hull.

They were back where they had started from and, when he sacked Colin after a few months, Don decided he had had enough of Hull City and went back to his first love, up the coast at Scarborough. We still exchange Christmas cards.

Dennis Booth (Hull City 1980–1988)

I first came across Brian when I was playing for Lincoln and he was at Port Vale, who were one of the dirtiest teams I have ever faced. When you came in at half-time, even the tea lady kicked you and you had to commit murder to get booked. You knew when you went to Vale Park that you had to stand up to them. I hated playing Nobby. He was very competitive.

I moved to Hull in 1980 and at the end of the season we had to go to Burnley and win by three clear goals to earn promotion. We won but only by two goals. It was a terrible mood in the dressing room. I had just given an interview to the radio. Colin Appleton told me to get the lads together and told them he was leaving and his assistant would be going with him. Billy Whitehurst turned to me and said: 'Looks like you're in charge, Dennis.'

My first instructions were that we should stay in the bar at Turf Moor and have a right good drink because, although we had missed out on promotion to the Second

Division, we had had a good season and we should celebrate it.

The chairman, Don Robinson, rang the next day and offered me a job as a coach and told me he would be looking to bring in a new manager as quickly as possible. Later, he asked me to take Hull to America to play in a tournament and halfway through he said:

'The new manager's coming over.'

'Who is it?'

'It's Brian Houghton.'

'Do you mean Brian Horton?'

'Yes, that's the one. He'll be a player-manager. He's a centre-half.'

'No, he's a midfield player.'

'Do you know him, then?'

'Yes, we used to kick the shit out of one another.'

Under Colin Appleton, Hull had been a very disciplined side; we would play balls into the channels. However, under Brian we were more adventurous, more attacking. I thought at one stage we would go straight from the Third Division to the top flight. It was a real mistake for the chairman to have sacked Brian when he did because we never recovered from it. I still do some corporate work at Hull City and a lot of people still talk about that era.

When Brian was player-manager, I would organise things from the sidelines, although since you only had one sub in those days there were not a lot of changes you could make. Nobby would shout something over or I would shout something to him.

We had Billy Whitehurst and Frankie Bunn up front and a lot of teams could not handle them. They were the best two forwards in the league and when the ball was crossed into them, no centre-half enjoyed it. Billy was feared. When we played the ball wide and were about to put it in, he would turn to their bench and shout: 'Get the stretcher ready.' There was at least one centre-half who would get out of the way when the ball came in from a corner.

Billy came to Hull from non-league. Colin Appleton had bought him from Mexborough for £2,000 and when he first came into the gym, I thought he had won a competition to train with us for the day. However, Chris Chilton, who was Colin's assistant, did a lot of work with him and made Billy into a proper centre-forward.

You had to know how to handle Billy because, if you tried to bully him, it would not work. We were in the bath one day and I said to him: 'Okay Billy, you can beat me up but what is knocking seven kinds of shit out of me going to prove?'

I think Billy liked me which was a major bonus because if he decided he didn't like you, that was it. He was not going to change his mind. He was the toughest player I have ever come across but I think he appreciated my silly jokes so we got on.

The Maxwell House

(Games 767–1,024)

THE Thames was glittering below me. It was a perfect autumn day and you could see the river as it snaked through London towards Oxford. I was flying in Robert Maxwell's helicopter several storeys above the skyline. I had just been asked to manage one of his football clubs, Oxford United. I was feeling physically sick.

It wasn't that I was terrified of working for the Maxwells or that I didn't feel I could do the job. I had an abiding fear of helicopters.

When I was taken to the roof of the Mirror Building, which was part of the Maxwell empire, there was a helicopter waiting to take me to Headington Hill Hall, the Maxwell family home. From there I would go straight to the Manor Ground, take charge of the team and take them back down to London to play Crystal Palace that evening.

Like its owner, Robert Maxwell's helicopter was big. The pilot said: 'Come and sit with me.' I had never been in a helicopter before in my life and the sweat was pouring from me. The journey must have taken no more than half an hour and I hated every minute of it.

Robert Maxwell's main business, Pergamon Press, was based in Oxford and in 1982 he had taken over Oxford United, planning to merge it with Reading to create a new club called Thames Valley Royals, which would be based in Didcot.

The plan came to nothing but, with Jim Smith as manager, Maxwell proved a successful chairman, taking Oxford from the Third to the First Division. In 1986, they won the League Cup.

The following year, Robert Maxwell took over Derby who also went from the Third to the First Division. He became chairman at the Baseball Ground while his son, Kevin, became chairman of Oxford.

In May 1988, I had been out of work for a month when I got a call from Mark Lawrenson, who had just been appointed manager of Oxford United.

They were in the First Division but had already been relegated and Mark wanted me to take a look at the team and tell him what I thought. It was the last Saturday of the season and they were at Nottingham Forest.

Oxford lost, 5-3, but they were playing against a club that finished third in 1988, behind Liverpool and Manchester United, and they could have won the game. Oxford had not won a league match for six months but they had reached the semi-finals of the League Cup, where they were beaten by Luton.

They had some good players; an attack led by Dean Saunders and Martin Foyle and Trevor Hebberd in midfield. I told Lawro that, if he managed to keep that team together, Oxford would go straight back up. I'd been in the Second Division for three seasons and I knew the level.

Later in the summer, Lawro called again and wondered if I'd join the club for pre-season because Mark had never done any coaching. I told him I wouldn't sign a contract with Oxford because I wanted to be a manager again but I would help out.

Pre-season went well; we had a good win at Swansea and beat Derby, a club who were managed by Arthur Cox. Dean Saunders scored the goal and played magnificently. The partnership between Dean and Martin Foyle was probably the best in the division but Saunders only had a year left on his contract.

Mark spoke to Kevin Maxwell and they agreed a new three-year contract. The season began well. We beat Hull and Brighton and drew with Chelsea and Leicester before results became more uneven but Dean was in superb form.

I said to Mark: 'I guarantee you that Arthur Cox will be on the phone from Derby asking for Dean.'

On 22 October, Mark was in his office at the Manor Ground while we prepared to face Blackburn. The phone rang and it was Kevin Maxwell on the line. 'You have to sell Dean Saunders to Derby for £1m.'

Mark sought me out and said: 'If the Maxwells tell me to sell Dean Saunders, I'm resigning.' I told him not to be so stupid. We should take the money. In 1988 there were a few decent players you could buy for a million quid if you were in the Second Division.

Mark was determined to force the issue and Kevin summoned us down to the Mirror Building at Holborn Circus.

If you went down to London to see him, the most you would get with Kevin Maxwell would be five or ten minutes. We went to the top floor of the Mirror Building. Kevin put me in one room and Mark in another.

After five minutes Kevin came in and informed me he was paying Mark off. Mark had offered his resignation but he was told he was being sacked, presumably on the grounds that nobody resigned on the Maxwells.

Kevin said he had done some research on me and would like to offer me the job. Oxford had a game at Crystal Palace that night and I asked if I could take the team to Selhurst Park and give him an answer in the morning.

'No, I want to know now. There is a phone on the desk, I'll give you 15 minutes to ring who you want.'

On the way down to London, Mark told me that if I wanted to stay and take his job, it would be fine by him. It would not be something we would fall out over.

I rang David Pleat, who was then managing Leicester. I rang Colin Brennan who was my accountant, whom I'd met when I was at Brighton for some financial advice. They both told me to take the job.

I rang my wife. We were still living in North Ferriby, the kids were in school and I couldn't commute to Oxford from Humberside. Denise's attitude was that they would go where I went. I told Kevin I would take the job. The salary would be £80,000.

The problem was that the players would be coming to the Manor Ground that afternoon to travel to London for the Crystal Palace game. They had heard the rumours about Mark Lawrenson going and Dean Saunders being sold and they would want to know what was going on.

I wondered how I was going to fit this in until Kevin said: 'Dad's helicopter is on the roof. Why don't you take that?' I arrived at the Manor Ground, gathered the troops, some of whom were in shock that Mark had left, and went to Crystal Palace, where we lost, 1-0. It was not the most auspicious of starts.

One of the reasons Mark Lawrenson had resigned was that he doubted whether we would ever see the £1m for Dean Saunders but Kevin Maxwell insisted Derby would pay the full amount and they did.

The money was to be my foundations for building a team of my own. I brought in Steve Foster, whom I'd played with at Brighton and knew very well. He would be in his thirties by then.

He had left Brighton in 1984 for Aston Villa, where little went right and I remember getting a call from David Pleat about him.

David said: 'I hear he likes a bet.'

I said: 'So do I.'

'But he likes a drink as well, doesn't he?'

'So do I, but I'll tell you something, David, he'll give you the same kind of team spirit you had from me. What fee are Aston Villa asking?'

'£350,000.'

'Bite their hand off because, for that, you get a ready-made captain.'

He went to Luton and captained them to the 1988 and 1989 League Cup finals after which I signed him to play for Oxford. It was a no-risk deal. You knew exactly what you were going to get for your money.

To play alongside him, I signed Andy Melville from Swansea in the summer of 1990. It went to a tribunal and we paid £275,000 which was a lot less than Swansea had been demanding. Andy was a terrific defender who would play nearly 70 times for Wales.

One day a lad from Oxford University turned up. He was 6ft 3in tall, a man mountain from New Zealand and asked if he could have a trial. His name was Ceri Evans.

His father, Gwyn, who was from the Rhondda Valley, had played for Crystal Palace before emigrating. Ceri had a degree in medicine from Otago University and was now at Oxford studying psychology.

Like his father, Ceri was a central defender and I paired him with Steve Foster from whom he learnt a lot about the professional game. Ceri was a quiet lad but very strong. Fozzie was a born leader who pulled the rest of his defence around him.

Trevor Hebberd joined Dean Saunders at Derby in part exchange for Mickey Lewis, who was to spend 27 years as a player and coach at Oxford.

I signed Jim Magilton and John Durnin from Liverpool. Neither had been able to break into the first team but I had faced them at Boothferry Park when Liverpool Reserves played Hull.

There are times when you are playing against someone, especially if you are playing against someone young, when you are startled by how good they are. You think to yourself: 'I like the look of you.'

I kept tabs on them and rang Kenny Dalglish to ask about Magilton and he said: 'Yes, a hundred grand. His contract's up in the summer. If you take us to a tribunal, I will make it very hard for you but for £100,000 you can have him.'

Jim was from Belfast, and was one of the best midfielders Oxford have ever had. His passing was exceptional, he had an eye for goal and he could take free kicks.

I'd been following Paul Simpson, who was at Manchester City, since he was a kid and nearly signed him for about £10,000, when Billy McNeill was manager at Maine Road.

However, by 1988 he was an England Under-21 international and had played two seasons for City in the top flight. His value was now £200,000. Paul had four years at Oxford and we sold him to Derby for three times what we had paid Manchester City. He would go on to manage England Under-20s to win the World Cup in South Korea.

Robert Maxwell was someone I only met once. I was with some of Oxford's directors in the Mirror Building, where we were due to meet Kevin. As usual, his secretary warned us we would be lucky to have ten minutes with him and, as we were waiting, Robert Maxwell burst into the room.

Pat McGeough, who was the club's chief executive, said: 'Mr Maxwell, this is Brian Horton.'

'I know who it is,' Maxwell boomed. 'He is doing a damned fine job and you had better give him the help he needs.' With that, he swept out.

My dealings were with Kevin. Robert Maxwell worked his sons very hard; Kevin had seven children so any time for Oxford United would be strictly limited.

He occasionally went to home games but he would never see us play away. There would be a conversation on the Monday about how the weekend had gone but there would be very little interference.

Because I had been a manager and a director at Hull, I had a good idea of how a football club worked by the time I came to the Manor Ground. Kevin asked if I did the transfers at Hull and, on that basis, he let me carry on negotiating the fees at Oxford.

When we had a transfer to conclude, I would phone Kevin and say: 'I'd like to buy Paul Simpson from Manchester

City. The fee is £250,000. I've tried to get him for less but they won't go lower.'

He would invariably say: 'Give me five minutes.' I don't know if it was to phone his dad or contact the bank but he would come back and say whether you could do it or not.

On the pitch, we struggled for consistency at Oxford. Seventeenth in 1989. Seventeenth in my first full season and then tenth in 1991. We had the AGMs in the social club behind one of the goals at the Manor Ground. Kevin took questions and I was alongside him on the top table.

One of the supporters stood up and said: 'I want to ask about Brian Horton's position at the club. Oxford are not doing well. Will there be a change of manager?'

Kevin replied: 'This is an AGM. I am not here to talk about Brian Horton, who is doing a fine job in difficult circumstances. There are no issues with him.'

Ten minutes later another supporter put his hand up and said: 'I think we have every right to ask questions about Brian Horton.'

Kevin stood up and replied: 'I am chairman of this football club and I am very happy with Brian Horton. We – the Maxwell Communications Corporation – own Oxford United and, if we pull our money out, this club will fold. That is the end of the discussion.'

At the end of the evening, he turned to me and said: 'Do you want to buy me a pint of bitter, then?'

Naturally, when I took the job, I had to move the family from North Ferriby. I found a house in Woodstock, on the edge of Blenheim Park, famed for its hotel, The Bear, where years before I had my honeymoon and where a long time later, in 1989, I celebrated my 40th birthday.

I'd become a neighbour of Jim Smith, who had moved to Woodstock, one of Oxfordshire's most beautiful towns, when he was in charge at the Manor Ground. Despite going on to manage Queens Park Rangers, Newcastle, Portsmouth and Derby, Jim had kept his home there.

We lived on a new development; beautiful five-bedroomed houses made out of Cotswold stone. I'd seen them being built and went over to the show home where a woman told me that if I gave her £50 there and then as a deposit, the house was mine. I still had to sort a mortgage but it was a very quick deal.

The house remains one of my biggest regrets about Oxford United. I should have done what Jim Smith did and kept it after I'd left the club. Instead, I sold it for exactly the same price – £265,000 – that I'd paid for it five years before.

It was the time of Black Friday and negative equity and nobody then was making money on property. Had I held on to it, the house would now be worth about a million pounds.

As a manager of a club like Oxford, you spent a lot of time on the road, watching reserve games, hoping to see someone who might spark your interest. I was given a black Rover Sterling and Kevin gave me a number plate to put on it which was 5OUFC. I said: 'Kevin, I don't want a personal number plate because it will just attract attention.' However, he insisted.

In January 1991 we beat Chelsea at Stamford Bridge in the FA Cup to set up a fourth-round tie at Tottenham. On the Wednesday before the tie, I drove down to White Hart Lane to see them play Chelsea in the League Cup. When I came out of the ground the bonnet of the Rover had been scratched to pieces. When I told Kevin, he replied: 'You can get it resprayed, can't you?'

We lost 4-2 at White Hart Lane. Paul Gascoigne had a hand in all four Spurs goals and scored twice. Martin Foyle scored both of Oxford's goals.

A couple of weeks later, on the way back from training, I took the car into the Manor Ground. I needed a few minutes to speak to the secretary or the chief executive and parked it behind a milk float. When I was in the office, I heard an almighty crunch.

The milk float had reversed over the bonnet. The driver was apologetic, explaining this was his first day driving it. I told him that at this rate it would be his last. The car was beyond rescuing with a respray. It needed a new bonnet, wing and front light. When they saw the wrecked Rover, you can imagine the players' reaction. They were delighted.

The worst company cars I had in my career came from Manchester City. The first was a Saab, who sponsored the club. I was travelling from my home in Woodstock to Manchester when, as I was driving past Stafford on the M6,

I flicked off the cruise control. All the electrics on the car failed and I just managed to get it into a layby before it came to a complete halt.

City then provided me with a white Ford Granada estate, which from a distance looked remarkably like an ambulance. I told them it should have come with two flashing blue lights.

When I was assistant to Mark Lawrenson, we went up to watch Glasgow Rangers play Hibernian in a pre-season fixture which they won 7-0.

We were interested in Jimmy Phillips, a defender who realistically was not quite good enough for the top-class side Graeme Souness was assembling at Ibrox but would be very good for Oxford. We had a glass of wine with Graeme and did a deal for £110,000. In 1990, Colin Todd bought Jimmy to Middlesbrough for more than double that.

It was while travelling back from a reserve game at Aston Villa with David Moss that we realised everything at Oxford United was about to change. It was 5 November 1991 and news came on the radio that Robert Maxwell had been lost at sea while on his yacht *Lady Ghislaine* which had been sailing around the Canary Islands.

I then had a phone call from Kevin, who said: 'Dad's gone missing and the money has to stop tonight. The sponsored cars have to go back and the mobile phones have to be returned. There's no money.' He added: 'Look, if you need a car, go down to Pergamon Press first thing in the morning and there are a few cars we do own outright.'

When it was confirmed that Robert Maxwell was dead and news came through that the Maxwell Communications Corporation was heading towards bankruptcy, owing more than £400m, it needed more than the cars going back to save the club. Almost every player that could be sold had to be sold.

Derby had been part of the Maxwell empire but it had been sold to Lionel Pickering, who published local newspapers, just before his death.

The Derby manager, Arthur Cox, was safe from the financial tidal wave that was engulfing Oxford but because of the Maxwell connection he knew everything about our club. He was straight on the phone asking to buy Paul Simpson for £650,000.

Oxford were not just in trouble financially. On the night of Robert Maxwell's death, we were second-bottom in Division Two. Derby were seventh, five points behind the leaders, Middlesbrough. I could not afford to sell anyone.

I was asked to see Pat McGeough, who said: 'We have had an offer from Derby County for Paul Simpson. Why haven't you told us?'

'Because I don't want to sell him.'

'You have no choice.'

Some time after that, I had another phone call from Arthur Cox. He came straight to the point: 'Jim Magilton, £750,000 – and if you don't tell Kevin, I will.'

I gave Arthur a piece of my mind down the phone but I was soon in Pat McGeough's office trying to stop the transfer. I asked him to get Kevin Maxwell on the phone.

I told Kevin: 'If we sell Jim Magilton, we will get relegated. He is my best player. There are only a few weeks of the season left and, if he goes, the dressing room will not be able to take it. We'll be down.'

He said: 'Give me five minutes.'

Goodness knows what he did or who he called but he came back to me and said: 'He can stay.'

By the time the final weekend of the season came around, Oxford were still in the relegation zone, third from bottom. Ironically, Magilton would not be available for the critical final game at Tranmere.

Our penultimate away game had been at Plymouth, one of our rivals for the drop to the Third Division. Not only had we lost 3-1 at Home Park but Jim had got himself sent off by David Elleray for swearing.

Peter Shilton was Plymouth's player-manager and, as we had a drink afterwards, you could sense that he thought they were safe. We had two matches left. Our last home game would be against Ipswich, who would be promoted to the newly formed Premier League as champions. Then we would have to go to Merseyside to play Tranmere. It looked bleak.

David Moss was showing symptoms of the flu. The last thing I wanted was it to spread to the squad so I asked him to make his own way back to Oxford.

Halfway up the M5, I told the coach driver to pull over and find a pub and I bought the lads some drinks. I'd had a go at them at Plymouth, Jim was especially down because he'd been sent off and I felt the team could do with some cheering up.

Our last game at the Manor Ground was against Ipswich, who needed a point to win promotion. The ground was sold out, Magilton scored but Ipswich battered us. We drew 1-1 and but for our goalkeeper, a big Northern Irishman called Paul Kee, we would have been thrashed.

On the final weekend of the season, Port Vale were bottom and relegated. Two clubs from five could join them in the third tier – Brighton and Oxford, who had 47 points, Plymouth, on 48, and Newcastle on 49. Grimsby could theoretically go down but they had 50 points and would only be relegated if they lost to Port Vale and everyone else won by a lot.

Our job on the last day was to better Plymouth's result. They were at home but they would be playing Blackburn, who had been taken over by Jack Walker and were being massively funded to break into the Premier League. Kenny Dalglish was now their manager and they needed something from the game to make the play-offs.

I had been given permission to take the team up to Merseyside on the Friday and we stayed at the Village Hotel in Birkenhead. There was a park pitch nearby and I thought I would get the players out on it.

It was probably the worst pitch I have ever set foot on. It sloped both ways and the players wondered what we were doing on it. This was something I'd learned from David Pleat, who was always keen not to let his footballers dwell on things. I did not want my players stuck in their hotel rooms thinking about the game.

There were about 1,500 Oxford fans at Prenton Park to watch a match that ebbed and flowed dramatically. Joey Beauchamp, a young, very talented Oxford lad, missed several chances, Paul Kee kept Tranmere out and in the second half, John Durnin put us ahead, which saw the Oxford fans spill on to the pitch.

The lead lasted a few minutes, before John Aldridge scored his 40th goal of the season to break Tranmere's goalscoring record. Then, Mickey Lewis passed to Beauchamp who shot through Eric Nixon's legs to give Oxford a 2-1 lead which we held on to until the end.

That, however, was not the end of matters. Brighton had lost, 3-1, at the champions, Ipswich, and had been relegated. Grimsby were safe and Newcastle had saved themselves with a 2-1 win at Leicester. That just left Plymouth.

Blackburn had taken so many fans down to Devon that kick-off had to be delayed for 15 minutes. We waited by the side of the pitch until a roar from the Oxford fans told us Plymouth had lost and we were safe. Blackburn would beat first Derby and then Leicester to reach the Premier League through the play-offs.

In the away dressing room at Prenton Park we only had tea to toast our success until somebody found a bottle of champagne. There was plenty of beer on the coach back.

Oxford had done astonishingly well to survive and a key to that had been the spirit of the players. They could have been overwhelmed by the collapse of the Maxwell empire; they could have accepted that the finances were so bad there was nothing they could do to save the club.

People like Mickey Lewis, Jim Magilton and John Durnin were all characters who refused to shrug their shoulders and let Oxford go under.

It was probably the biggest game of my managerial career. If we had lost, Oxford would have been relegated. The club would have been taken over and I would almost certainly have got the sack. I might not have got another job. In football, sometimes you don't get another job.

An ankle injury had forced Steve McClaren to retire at the end of the season and I offered him what would be his first coaching job. Steve was a good holding midfielder, who was a fine passer of the ball and I had managed him at Hull and Oxford.

At neither club was it obvious he would end up in coaching. There were some players – Jim Magilton, for example – who you knew would become managers but I offered Steve the post of youth-team manager and he took to it fantastically.

He learned a lot from Maurice Evans, who was then the club's general manager. Maurice had come to Oxford from Reading, where he'd been a player and a manager, to run the youth team and be the club's chief scout.

He had taken over when Jim Smith quit to join Queens Park Rangers. He had then beaten Jim when Oxford played QPR in the 1986 League Cup Final.

Maurice had resigned just before Oxford's relegation but he stayed at the club and he and I shared an office at the Manor Ground. The Maxwells loved him, Maurice was a proper football man and Steve would come to the office and talk to us both.

The following year, I made Steve reserve-team coach. He said to me once: 'Don't come to the games, gaffer. You always want us to win, you're wound up and you have a go – and that's not what some young players need.'

It was a point I understood and accepted and it was the sort of thinking that made Steve McClaren into a very fine coach.

When, in 1993, I was offered the manager's job at Manchester City, I took David Moss with me. I was thinking of adding Steve to the coaching staff at Maine Road but I didn't want to cause Oxford too much disruption and never made the offer.

Had I done so, things might have worked out very differently. Steve went to Derby to work as Jim Smith's number two. They won promotion to the Premier League in 1996 and three years later he was at Old Trafford working alongside Alex Ferguson and winning the Champions League.

In the summer of 1992, Oxford United was taken over by a recycling company called Biomass. They told me that I would be taking instructions directly from the chief executive, Pat McGeough. I had a decent enough relationship with Pat, whose father had been my parents' doctor back in Cannock.

However, I was not prepared to follow his orders on the football side of the business and I told my wife, Denise, I thought this might be the end for us at Oxford.

In the end, they relented and I was told I could carry on as I had done under the Maxwells. There was very little money and it would be a long slog to survive. Oxford finished 14th in 1993, which given the finances of the club was a considerable achievement.

Although we could not afford to buy very much, in Chrissy Allen and Joey Beauchamp we had two excellent products of Oxford's youth system. Chrissy was from the Blackbird Leys estate, which had been the centre of rioting in the summer of 1991 and where Oxford United's new stadium now stands. Nottingham Forest would pay £600,000 to make him a Premier League midfielder.

Joey was an outstanding footballer. He lived with his parents near the Manor Ground and all he ever wanted to do was play for Oxford United. He could play on either wing, he possessed wonderful ball control and a real eye for goal.

I turned down an offer of £1m from Wolverhampton Wanderers for Joey but after I'd left to go to Manchester City, Oxford were relegated to the third tier. The club could not afford to keep him and sold him to West Ham for £1m.

Joey was an Oxford boy; his life was in the city. He liked going into the social club at the Manor with his mum, dad and girlfriend. He was shy and insular but when he got on a football pitch the talent was there for everyone to see.

Billy Bonds, who was then the manager at Upton Park, told him he could commute from Oxford. Joey found that impossible and he could not face the thought of living in London. He lasted 58 days at West Ham and was transferred to Swindon before he could play a competitive game for the club.

The 1992/93 season was my ninth as a manager. All but one had been in the Championship. I'd won Hull promotion and taken them to one of the highest finishes in their history. While there had been no records broken at Oxford, I had kept them afloat through one of the most turbulent periods of their existence.

It was now that I was offered the chance to manage in the Premier League. I was 44 years old. I felt I had earned it, that I had done my apprenticeship. The reaction when I joined Manchester City was: Brian who?

Mark Lawrenson (manager Oxford United 1988)

The problem at Oxford United was Daddy Maxwell. I quite liked Kevin and everything we asked him for we got, more or less. Robert was at Derby and simply told Kevin that Dean Saunders was going to the Baseball Ground.

We had just got Dean to sign a new three-year contract and told him that, if we didn't get ourselves back into the big league, he could leave. There were loads of clubs interested in him, there would have been no problem finding him a club.

What made it more difficult was that Arthur Cox was the manager at Derby and I had known him since I was 14 because he had been assistant to Alan Ball Senior, when I was at Preston. I used to be a left-winger then and he would join in training on a Tuesday night and kick the shit out of me. One night I kicked him back. Arthur said: 'My work here is done,' turned around and left.

Coxy came to almost every Oxford game he could to watch Dean and then just before we faced Blackburn, Kevin called me to say that I wasn't to play Saunders because he would be talking to Derby at the end of the game.

I said to Brian: 'Bollocks to that, Nobby. He's playing.'

At the end of the match I told Dean he was free to speak to Derby, although this being football, he had already spoken to them.

If the Maxwells had said, 'We want to sell Saunders,' I would have replied: 'Give us two weeks and allow us to buy two or three replacements with the money we are going to get for him.' This was because once Dean Saunders went the price for any replacement would go up because everyone knew Oxford had a million quid to spend.

That night, Kevin rang me and said: 'The Saunders deal is done.'

I told him I felt very let down. He said: 'It's not me, it's my father. He is in the Mirror Building tomorrow, why don't you come down and see us.'

I tried to resign but Kevin ended up sacking me and it took him eight-and-a-half months to pay me. His dad had gone off to the States to buy the *New York Daily News* on board *Lady Ghislaine* and nothing was decided without him.

The club had a director called John Devaney. Under the Maxwells the directors at Oxford had no power whatsoever, they just paid more for their seats than anybody else.

John took over Peterborough and in 1989 I became the club's manager. He was a builder and he had a big development in Weston-super-Mare which he had financed by borrowing a lot of money. Then the Stock Market crashed.

I had four experienced players, including George Berry, who used to play for Wolves. The deal I had with them was that they would double their money if they played in the first team but, if I had any doubts about their attitude, I would drop them to the reserves. This was my insurance against them coming to Peterborough and taking the piss.

John Devaney, whose wife basically ran the club, made a rare appearance one Thursday and said we should play the kids. I told him we didn't have any that were good enough for league football but he insisted we could not play experienced pros. I did not know about the crash in Weston-super-Mare and so I said: 'You and your wife can run the team.' I didn't manage again.

David Moss (assistant manager, Oxford United 1988–1993)

I loved coaching the young players at Oxford, especially Joey Beauchamp. Nowadays people think they have reinvented the game when they play a left-footed right-winger but we did that at Oxford with Joey, who was one of the first left-footed right-wingers. I knew how that could work because at Luton I was a right-footed left-winger.

When Robert Maxwell died, we had to dig in together. I rang Brian and said: 'They have taken the car off me. I can't get to work.' He said: 'Get on the bus like anybody else.' I think it galvanised us. We survived, I don't know how. Lee Nogan had to be sold to Watford straight away to pay the wages.

As he was as a player, Brian was very demanding as a manager. Some of the Manchester City players did not know how to take it. Brian could be very straight with the players. Sometimes, he would say to me: 'Pick them up and have a laugh with them.'

When I came up to Manchester, I didn't buy a house because the job was simply not secure enough. We lived in hotels for about three months but I hadn't long been married so I had to make a decision to buy a place just outside Lymm in Cheshire. I have lived there ever since.

Citizen

(Games 1,025–1,121)

WHO are you? What have you done? Some of the players have never heard of you.

Some of the questions at my first press conference as manager of Manchester City were, frankly, insulting. I had captained two teams in what would now be the Premier League for five seasons and been a manager in what would now be the Championship for nine.

In the press room at Maine Road, I thought to myself: 'If you don't know I captained the Luton side that relegated you at Maine Road in 1983, where have you been?' It was before the age of Sky Sports and rolling football news but, even so, the degree of ignorance was profound.

Those attitudes have hardened. When Frank Lampard moved from Derby to Chelsea in the summer of 2019 it was the first time in 12 years that an English manager had moved from a Championship club to one in the Premier League. That appointment may have been more than partly due to Lampard's status as one of Chelsea's greatest players.

Usually, the only way to become a Premier League manager from the Championship is to promote the club you run. Perhaps the success of Chris Wilder, who took Sheffield United from League One to the top flight, might change those perceptions.

The approach from Manchester City had been out of the blue. In 1993 Manchester United had won the title for the first time in 26 years which increased the pressure on the manager, Peter Reid, and escalated the protests against the chairman, Peter Swales.

The season had finished with a 5-2 home defeat to Everton and now City had taken one point from their opening four matches. It was then that I received a phone call from John Maddock, who had worked for Robert Maxwell at the *Sunday People* and whom I had known since my time at Port Vale.

John was a powerful journalist with many, many connections in the game and often acted as the link man between a chairman and a potential new manager. Swales had appointed him general manager at Manchester City to deal with the day-to-day running of the club.

I was in my office at the Manor Ground when in August 1993 I received a call from John. Manchester City had just lost 2-0 at home to Blackburn and I was told a decision had been made to sack Peter Reid.

My attitude to that news was the same as it has been throughout my managerial career. I told John I would not discuss the position until I had assurances that Reid had gone. Talking to a club while a manager is in place is something that I and many of my generation have absolutely frowned upon.

I was told Peter had definitely gone and would I like to talk about taking over at Maine Road? I suggested we met at Tillington Hall in Staffordshire, where Luton had stayed the weekend they had relegated Manchester City in 1983.

I met John Maddock and City's vice-chairman, Freddie Pye, who was a scrap-metal merchant who had been, initially, sceptical about appointing me.

On the Friday, I came up to Manchester to meet Peter Swales and finalise the contract, which would pay me £120,000 a year – £40,000 more than I had been paid at Oxford. That evening, City, with Tony Book as caretaker, were at home to Coventry. David Moss watched the game in the Platt Lane End. The match was drawn 1-1. The atmosphere was bad but nothing like as venomous as it was to become.

Manchester City were on the brink of civil war. Francis Lee, who had been one of the men who had made City one of the biggest clubs in Britain between 1967 and 1972 and was now a highly successful businessman, was preparing a takeover. One of Peter Swales's first pieces of advice to me was that I should not buy a house in Manchester. My job would not be secure enough to justify it.

I also needed to win over the dressing room quickly. A lot of the players were close to Peter Reid and had been angered by his sacking. Relations between Peter and me were a little frosty after his dismissal but we are fine now. David White wanted to leave. I soon realised that Niall Quinn was the key member of the dressing room which was full of strong characters like Tony Coton, Steve McMahon and Keith Curle, who I needed to get on board.

I decided to keep Tony Book on the staff. Tony was a bigger figure at Manchester City than I was. He had captained them to the championship and the FA Cup and managed them to the League Cup and second place in the league in 1977. Nine years later, as youth-team manager, he had beaten Manchester United to win the FA Youth Cup.

I had first met Tony at Lilleshall, where the FA used to put on coaching courses for managers and coaches. You would stay for three or four days, watch some training routines, listen to some lectures from the likes of Bobby Robson and, almost as importantly, you would talk to each other in the bar in the evening. I would have been in my early 30s and I found myself sharing a dormitory with Tony Book, who at the time was managing Manchester City.

There might have been some managers who would have been afraid of having someone like that near the dressing room and might have considered Tony a threat. I was never afraid of experience and Tony's advice proved invaluable. The players loved him and invariably called him 'Skip'.

I brought in Colin Bell to help run the youth team alongside Neil McNab for much the same reason. I wanted the young footballers at Manchester City to have an icon they could look up to. Francis Lee would sack both Colin and Tony.

Bernard Halford had run Maine Road as club secretary since 1972. Bernard organised everything off the field for Peter Swales, he was passionate about Manchester City and our relationship was one of the strongest I have known in football. He served the club for 39 years and became life president. Since his death, I still see his wife, Karen, and their family at the Etihad.

It was not just the dressing room I needed to get onside. There was the press, the people who claimed they had never heard of me. John Maddock told me he was getting complaints that the media found it difficult to get hold of me and needed to speak to me between press conferences.

He invited the press to Maine Road, we put some food and wine on and John told them they could have an hour with me. 'They can all ask for your phone number and, if they can't get you after that, they have no excuses.'

Generally, I got on well with the Manchester press corps but the problems came after Francis Lee had replaced Peter Swales. They knew I wasn't Francis's man and the questions every week tended to be a variation on: 'How long do you think you've got?' and 'What's going to happen if you lose tomorrow?' If Manchester City won, they would assume I would be at Maine Road for a few more weeks. Then the questions would start again.

My first game was on a Wednesday night at Swindon. I could not have handpicked a better game. It was not just that Swindon had started worse than Manchester City – they had taken one point from their opening five matches and would not win a league game until the end of November. Because of the County Ground's proximity to Oxford, they were a team I knew well and had often played against.

After winning promotion, Swindon had been destabilised by Glenn Hoddle's decision to move to Chelsea in the summer. However, their way of playing had not changed. They would play one up front with Jan-Age Fjortoft leading the attack and they would employ a sweeper system. I picked my team accordingly and City won, 3-1.

My first home game was a few days later, against Queens Park Rangers. It was the afternoon when Francis Lee officially launched his takeover bid for the club. Again, we won, 3-0. I had a problem with the right-back position and persuaded Garry Flitcroft to fill in. He protested he had never played there but not only did he play, he scored.

I then persuaded Peter Swales to give Garry a five-year contract. He was by then playing regularly in midfield for England Under-21s but City were paying him peanuts. Manchester City would sell him to Blackburn in 1996 for £2.8m.

Peter Swales was a man I found very easy to deal with. He was a passionate supporter of the club and he did not interfere in team matters, which is something that sometimes could not be said for the man who succeeded him, Francis Lee.

Swales asked if I had negotiated the transfers at Hull and Oxford. I told him that Don Robinson and Kevin Maxwell had trusted me implicitly. That was fine by Swales. He had negotiated the deals in the past but now he was becoming weary of it all.

There was usually pressure to raise money. Early on in my time at Maine Road, Peter Swales asked me to meet Stephen Boler, who was the major shareholder and owned the Mere Country Club in Cheshire, where Manchester City did a lot of its business.

Swales and Boler had a spreadsheet in front of them on which was laid out the Manchester City squad. They went through each player and asked if I would sell or keep them. 'Would you sell Tony Coton?' No. We kept on until we had gone through the playing staff.

My answer to most of the questions was 'no'. Peter Swales, who was looking to make some sales, said: 'You don't really want to sell anyone, do you? Frankly, the players you want to get rid of aren't going to make us much money.'

'No. We have the makings, the backbone of a really good squad. If we are going to be successful, we need to keep the squad together.'

Swales and Boler, who had put a lot of money into Manchester City, backed me. Sometimes, however, I had to insist that sales were not made. When I became manager, I was made aware of a deal to sell Steve Lomas to Preston for £100,000 plus a player.

Straight away, I phoned Preston's manager, John Beck, to tell him that no player he had at Deepdale was worth that exchange. Steve was not then a regular first-teamer but I had seen enough of him to know he was someone worth keeping and he formed an exceptional partnership in midfield with Garry Flitcroft. They were both footballers with real energy.

I made some changes like bringing in Eric Steele as goalkeeping coach. Eric went on to do the same role at Manchester United, coaching Edwin van der Sar and David de Gea. Eric had known about De Gea long before he became a star and was instrumental in his move from Atletico Madrid.

I had known Eric since my days at Brighton, when he vied for the goalkeeping jersey with Graham Moseley. If one of them made a mistake, Alan Mullery would select the other, much as England did with Ray Clemence and Peter Shilton. It was a policy that kept both men on their toes.

Robbie Brightwell, who had won a silver medal at the Tokyo Olympics in 1964 and who was the father of David and Ian – who were both at Manchester City – came in from time to time as a specialist fitness coach.

Some things you had little control over as manager. The redevelopment of the Kippax, which cost £16m, forced me to sell Mike Sheron to Norwich. I don't think the redeveloped stand ever had the atmosphere of the great old terrace and the vast new stand only lasted seven years until it was torn down with the rest of Maine Road in 2003.

There were odd times when Swales would intervene on transfers. We talked seriously about signing Chris Sutton from Norwich but he went to Blackburn, where he became a lethal strike partner for Alan Shearer.

As the season wore on, the demonstrations against Peter Swales became more intense. It must have had an effect on the team because sometimes the atmosphere at Maine Road was toxic. I tried not to let it affect me and attempted to protect the team as much as possible. Certainly, my relationship with the Manchester City fans was good. I like to think they supported what I was trying to do and I still appreciate the passion they have for the very different club that has brought league titles to the Etihad Stadium.

When Francis Lee had taken over as chairman in 1994, we made a serious attempt to bring Luis Figo to Maine Road. He was playing for Sporting Lisbon, a club that Malcolm Allison had managed to the Portuguese championship in 1982.

Malcolm was living in Middlesbrough at the time but, under Franny, he became a frequent visitor to the boardroom at Maine Road, where he would hold court with his cigars and his champagne – and he still had some good contacts in Portugal.

David Pleat once told me that, win or lose, as a manager you should always go to the boardroom after a game. You should not swerve the chairman when you lose or gain a reputation for only showing your face after a victory.

It was in the boardroom that Malcolm asked me: 'Have you ever seen Luis Figo play?' I told him I hadn't. This was before the days when you could watch every foreign league on satellite television. 'Check him out,' said Malcolm. 'He is going to be an absolute star.'

I asked my secretary, Julia McKenzie, to find out where Figo was playing next. It turned out that Portugal were due to play Northern Ireland in Belfast. Tony Book and I went over to Windsor Park to see Portugal win, 2-1, with Figo, who was then 21, turning in an astonishing performance.

When I returned to Manchester, I told Francis Lee that City should do whatever it took to get him. We made contact with Figo's agents – he had several – and had a meeting with them at the Stanneylands Hotel, which was opposite Francis's home near Manchester Airport. The fee would have been £1.2m.

We came to the conclusion that the transfer was simply not viable. There were too many agents, each of whom wanted their cut, and there was a regulation that prevented Portuguese clubs selling their players to foreign teams during the season.

Barcelona managed to manoeuvre around that by agreeing a £2m fee with Sporting Lisbon and then loaning him back for the remainder of the season. Had we done the transfer it would have been quite a coup for Brian Who.

There were, however, some entertaining players who while not being Luis Figo, I was able to bring to Maine Road – Uwe Rösler, Paul Walsh, Nicky Summerbee and Peter Beagrie.

In January 1994, I tried to engineer a reunion with Paul Walsh, whom I had captained at Luton a decade before. He was now 32 and playing for Portsmouth in what would now be the Championship.

Portsmouth had back-to-back fixtures in the North West, an FA Cup tie with Blackburn, followed by a League Cup quarter-final at Old Trafford. They were staying at Mottram Hall in Cheshire and I went to see Jim Smith, Portsmouth's manager, to see if we could do a deal.

Over a glass of wine, Jim told me that Walshy was absolutely not for sale. Not long afterwards, Portsmouth's chairman, Jim Gregory, announced that there would have to be some serious cost-cutting at Fratton Park and that players would now have to be sold.

I offered Portsmouth £600,000 and invited Paul back up to Mottram Hall to sign the contract. Franny, the club secretary, Bernard Halford, and I were in the room when Walsh arrived with his agent, Eric Hall.

I asked him why he had brought his agent. 'I want him to get me a better deal.'

'Walshy, I know what you're on at Portsmouth. We are going to improve your contract and take you up a division. I know there is no way you are going to turn it down and there is absolutely no point in bringing Eric Hall here.'

I left them to talk money with Bernard and Franny and not long afterwards I was sharing a bottle of champagne with them all. I don't think Paul got his 'improved deal'.

Nicky Summerbee was brought in from Swindon after their relegation from the Premier League in 1994. I was pushing to bring him to Maine Road and was on holiday in the Forte Village in Cagliari when I had a phone call from Francis Lee.

Naturally, Franny was keen because Nicky was Mike Summerbee's son and the pair of them had played together when Manchester City had won the title in 1968.

Nicky was also a good winger and was attracting interest from Kenny Dalglish at Blackburn and from Bryan Robson at Middlesbrough, which was driving the price up towards £1.5m.

That was roughly my valuation of him and I told Franny that, if it went higher, he had every right to pull out of the deal. Despite Middlesbrough flying Nicky up to Teesside in a private jet to meet Bryan Robson, I pulled it off.

In terms of personality, Nicky Summerbee was the opposite of his father. He was a shy, quiet lad. Once, we were playing at Maine Road and Mike Summerbee was standing by the tunnel. Afterwards, someone said to me: 'Did you see Mike shouting instructions to Nicky?'

I hadn't but it left me furious. At the time Maine Road was being redeveloped and we were renting offices by the Princess Parkway. On the Monday I asked if Mike would come to my office and I asked him if he had been shouting instructions to Nicky.

'I was only trying to help.'

'Mike, Nicky has got nothing to do with you any more. I am the one who should be giving him information. When he's out on the pitch, he is no longer your son, he is my player.'

To this day, Mike Summerbee maintains this was one of the biggest bollockings he had received in his life. Despite that, we have remained good friends.

On the opposite wing from Nicky was Peter Beagrie. Our original target had been Anders Limpar, who had won the title with Arsenal in 1991. However, Limpar had fallen out with George Graham and was looking to leave Highbury when his contract ended in the summer.

Francis Lee and I met Anders at Stanneylands and, when he left, we thought we had got him. However, he then decided to speak to Joe Royle at Everton who did the deal to bring him to Goodison Park.

However, that move put Beagrie's position under threat and, on deadline day, I asked Joe if we could arrange a transfer. It had to be done by five o'clock so Peter had to come over from Merseyside to Maine Road and make a swift decision. He said yes.

Uwe Rösler was probably my best signing at Manchester City. In March 1994 I took a phone call from the agent, Jerome Anderson, who asked me what I was looking for. Three months before, Niall Quinn had torn his cruciate ligaments playing against Sheffield Wednesday and I badly needed a striker.

Anderson told me he had an East German centre-forward called Uwe Rösler who was at Dynamo Dresden and would I be interested in taking him on trial? Uwe had been an East German international and it was quite unusual to be offered that calibre of footballer for a trial.

I decided to play Uwe in a reserve game against Burnley at Maine Road. Rösler scored twice and looked terrific. Maine Road on a reserve night was full of scouts and I turned to Franny and said: 'We should get him off now.'

I met Uwe in the boardroom with Franny and we offered him a short-term deal.

Since Quinn's injury, City had scored nine goals in 12 games and had won only three times.

We put Uwe straight into the team to play Queens Park Rangers at Loftus Road. He provided the cross that David Rocastle put away to earn us a 1-1 draw. The fans took to him immediately. They celebrated him in song and they adored his attitude.

As manager of Manchester City, you were introduced to some interesting people. One of those was Keith Pinner, who was a former policeman and passionate City supporter. He had founded a company called Arena International which was based in the little Cheshire town of Disley and brokered the sponsorship deals between the Premier League, Carling and Barclaycard.

Keith sold the business in 2008 for £2.7m and was made an honorary president of Manchester City. When he died, he left his body to science and no fewer than five former Manchester City managers – Tony Book, Peter Reid, myself, Frank Clark and Joe Royle – attended his memorial service at the Etihad Stadium. Sir Alex Ferguson also came while David Moyes, who was then manager of Real Sociedad, thought so much of Keith that he flew back from Shanghai to attend the service. His wife, Alma, and her family still support City at the Etihad.

Another influential character was Mike Marshall and his wife, Catriona. Mike worked for Mars, who became one of the FA's major sponsors. For those Mars employees who achieved their targets, he organised a trip to the 1994 World Cup. He asked me, Trevor Cherry, who had won the title with Leeds in 1974 and was now a successful businessman, and the referee, Neil Midgley, to come to Florida with them.

We watched Ireland beaten by Mexico in searing heat in Orlando and then did question-and-answer sessions with the Mars employees. Over the years, I have done a lot of these, mainly at supporters' branches and, despite what you might think from social media, the questions tend to be kind.

Fans usually want to ask about your best, rather than your worst moments. My stories tend to be about scoring the first goal at Newcastle in 1979 on the day Brighton went into the big time for the first time in their history or the agonising wait with my Oxford team at Tranmere as we learned whether we had survived the threat of relegation.

One of Neil Midgley's stories involved me and Steve Williams, who played midfield for Southampton and Arsenal. Hull were playing Southampton in the League Cup at The Dell and after five minutes Neil came up to us and said: 'I have left my wife in Manchester and instead of her nagging I have got yours. I am sick of it. This is the end.'

Manchester City ended up 16th in 1994, which was their lowest finish since they came back to the top flight five years before. However, considering they had taken two points from their opening five matches and the club had been in a state of civil war, relegation had been avoided reasonably comfortably.

On holiday in Sardinia I was excited by what lay ahead. We had assembled a very good forward line with Rösler and Walsh. Niall Quinn would be coming back to full fitness, Beagrie and Summerbee would supply the crosses. It was also an attack full of characters and full of spirit. The dressing room was united and I thought Maine Road would be an exciting place to watch football.

There was, however, one thought playing in the back of my mind. Whatever happened at Manchester City, however well I did, I thought I was unlikely to survive.

Francis Lee had completed his takeover in February 1994. He had inherited me as his manager and I knew he would want his own man. If I was to go down, I thought I would go down giving Maine Road the kind of football they wanted. We would attack.

There was no finer example of what I wanted than on 22 October at Maine Road when we overran Tottenham. Ossie Ardiles was in charge of Spurs at the time and I had a drink with him and his assistant, Steve Perryman, at Mottram Hall the night before the game.

The last time I'd faced Ardiles, managing Oxford against Newcastle, we had won 5-2 and Ossie had been sacked the next morning. This time the score was the same – 5-2 – and Ardiles lasted two more matches before his chairman, Alan Sugar, fired him.

John Motson once told me that this was one of the best games he had ever commentated on. Paul Walsh was absolutely motivated. He had left Tottenham after punching Ray Clemence, who was the club's reserve-team manager, and was desperate to prove a point while Peter Beagrie proved that on his day he was as good as any winger in the country.

Walshy was a very different player in 1994 than he had been in 1984. He had matured at Liverpool. Now he knew when to pass, when to dribble, when to lay the ball off. He had become a complete footballer and watching him excited me. David Pleat always used to say to us at Luton: 'I don't just want you to excite the crowd, I want you to excite me.'

Often in that 1994/95 season, City would play a very aggressive 4-2-4. It was easier to go forward because Steve McMahon, a central midfielder who played in much the same role as I had at Brighton, had gone to Swindon to become player-manager. He had exactly the right attributes

148

to be a manager and stayed at the County Ground for four years.

Maurizio Gaudino was one of my more interesting deals. He was a very talented midfielder who had won the Bundesliga title with Stuttgart in 1992 and was now at Eintracht Frankfurt who were offering him on loan.

The reason Frankfurt were keen to loan out Gaudino was because he had been implicated in a stolen car racket. Expensive cars were stolen to order, driven to eastern Europe and sold. A claim would then be made on the insurance. Had I known; I would probably have asked him to get me a Ferrari.

He made his debut in a League Cup tie at Newcastle, which City won, 2-0. It was the first time that Newcastle, under Kevin Keegan, had lost at St James' Park in 11 months.

His best performance came a few months later against Liverpool, who had just won the League Cup. We beat them, 2-1. Gaudino scored with a diving header and, when the final whistle went, he lay down flat on his back as Charlie George used to do whenever he scored for Arsenal.

This was on the Friday and we were due to play Blackburn, who were leading the Premier League, at Ewood Park on the Monday. I asked Stan Gibson, the groundsman at Maine Road, if we could train on the pitch. While we were there, the physio told me that Maurizio had gone down with flu which rather suited me because I had decided not to play him.

Gaudino was a free spirit in midfield which was fine when playing Liverpool, who then were a fluid, attacking team who were still celebrating winning at Wembley. It was quite another matter playing Maurizio at Ewood Park against a very disciplined, very effective Blackburn side that was pushing hard for the league title.

Francis Lee rang me on the Sunday night to ask what team I'd be playing at Blackburn. He was not happy with the selection and told me so. I stuck to the team I had picked. We went to Ewood Park and won, 3-2.

Francis did interfere, although not as much as many people might suppose. We had beaten Sheffield Wednesday 3-2, and then on the Tuesday night lost 2-0 at Wimbledon. Francis went into the dressing room at Selhurst Park to have a go at the players. What made it worse was he repeated, almost word for word, what I had just told the team.

In Francis's eyes, he had been a great player for Manchester City and was entitled to voice his opinion. I was also aware I was not his appointment. I had been Peter Swales's man.

However, at Hull and Oxford I had worked for two big personalities in Don Robinson and Kevin Maxwell. They had left me to run the team on the understanding that, if I messed up, I could expect the sack.

By then – March 1995 – I knew I would be finished when the season ended. I had learned that unless Manchester City finished in the top six, Franny would make a change. We were 12th when the final whistle went at Ewood.

I had decided I would not watch the Blackburn game from the dugout so I left Tony Book and David Moss on the bench and watched from the stands. I fancied us to play well and we did.

City were trailing 2-1 at half-time on a sodden night but first Uwe Rösler and then Paul Walsh scored to give us a victory we absolutely deserved. I met Kenny Dalglish and his assistant, Ray Harford, for a drink after the game and they both asked where this team had been all season. Blackburn hung on to take the title from Manchester United by a point.

This was one of the games I will remember all my life and because I knew I would probably not be starting another season with this team, I asked the coach driver to take us to the Haydock Thistle hotel, where we had stayed before the game.

I rang the hotel manager and asked if he could lay on some sandwiches and champagne. Some of the players were wondering why we were going and said they wanted to meet up with their wives. I told them to ask their wives to come to Haydock because I wanted to thank the players for what they had done and tell them I was unlikely to be at Maine Road next season.

To my mind we had the makings of a really good team. Uwe Rösler thought that with a couple of tweaks we would be a top six side.

In fact, Manchester City would be relegated in 1996, something I took absolutely no pleasure from. I knew and liked Alan Ball, the man Francis chose to succeed me. He had played for Southampton while I was at Brighton and we would meet at the racecourse at Fontwell. I told Alan he would have to manage the chairman as well as the team.

If I anticipated the sack, I was quite unprepared for the manner in which it was delivered. The final game of the season had seen Manchester City lose 3-2 at home to Queens Park Rangers.

I then went to the League Managers' Association annual dinner in St Albans. The next day I was coming down to breakfast at Sopwell House when I ran into Frank Clark, who had been voted manager of the year for taking a newly promoted Nottingham Forest to third in the Premier League.

'Are you okay?' Frank asked.

'I'm fine. Why do you ask?'

'Have you not seen the papers?'

I was the back-page lead in black and white. I had been dismissed as manager of Manchester City.

Straight away, I rang Julia, my secretary, and asked if she could get hold of Francis to ask him about the story but no answer was forthcoming. In the end, I managed to meet Francis at Stanneylands and he told me the stories were true and I had lost my job. He apologised for the way the sacking was leaked, although it would not have been a back-page story had he kept it to himself.

Curiously, Frank Clark, who had shown me the papers, would become manager of Manchester City and be dismissed by Francis in a very similar way. The first he knew that he was no longer manager was hearing the news on his car radio.

I had a 12-month rolling contract and Francis said he would pay up what was owing on it. However, six weeks later, I was appointed as manager of Huddersfield Town. Francis Lee argued that since I was now being paid by another club, I would not be due any compensation.

Manchester City took me to a tribunal and, although I was told by the LMA's barrister, who was representing me, that 'I couldn't lose', I lost. The judge ruled that I was not entitled to compensation because I had gone straight into another job on a salary that was not much lower than my wages at Manchester City.

Although I see him at games at the Etihad Stadium, I have not spoken to Francis Lee since. Once I had left, Francis made transfers which I could not fathom.

The sale of Garry Flitcroft to Blackburn in March 1996 knocked the bottom out of the club at a critical time. There was a real need to bring money into Manchester City but, had I still been in charge, it would have been a deal I would never have sanctioned.

If the deal had to be done, it should have waited until the end of the season.

Getting rid of Tony Coton not only deprived Manchester City of a top-class goalkeeper but a character who was a leader in the dressing room. The lads loved him.

Paul Walsh went back to Portsmouth in exchange for Gerry Creaney, which was wrong on two counts. Walsh may have been 33 but he was still an effective forward who had scored 15 goals in my last season at City. Creaney was no kind of replacement.

I felt I deserved more than the 20 months I was given at Manchester City. I had been managed by two men, Alan Mullery and David Pleat, who both demanded that their teams attacked and entertained. I like to think that the teams I sent out to perform in front of the Kippax did exactly that.

Uwe Rösler (Manchester City 1994–1998)

When I came to Manchester, Brian Horton didn't know me, Francis Lee didn't know me; they were taking a punt. I tell my son that while you need to work hard and you get nothing for free, you also need to be in the right place at the right time. I needed that bit of luck as well and I had that fortune.

I was supposed to have gone for a trial at Middlesbrough but the game was cancelled due to snow. I was on my way back to Germany when I got a call from my agent saying would you try out for Manchester City and I said 'yes'. Niall Quinn had done his cruciate ligaments and they needed a striker.

I had read a little bit about them and I knew they had a German connection because of Bert Trautmann. I played and scored in a reserve fixture against Burnley. Afterwards, Brian said he would like to give me a three-month contract with an option for another two or three years. That was okay with me and I was excited. It was something completely new for a German player to go to England and I wanted to see something of the culture and lifestyle. I scored five goals in 12 games.

I came into a team where there was a lot of experience, players who helped me understand British football culture. Because of my lack of English, I couldn't understand too much but Alfons Groenendijk and Michel Vonk, who were Dutch and understood both German and English, translated for me.

Brian bought me and Paul Walsh, David Rocastle and Peter Beagrie. Manchester City invested a lot in that period and it took two or three games for Paul Walsh and myself to form a partnership. Steve McMahon was a big help to me. He would take me to one side and give me advice on how to play the defenders I would be up against.

In my first two or three games with Paul, we played against very defensive teams in Wimbledon and Sheffield United. In the third game, Ipswich away, we scored. Paul and I needed to adapt to one another. We didn't talk much but eventually it clicked.

It took time because when I came to Manchester City, I needed fitness and match practice. I needed to get up to the speed of the game. The relationship I had with Paul Walsh was the best I ever had with a striker. We are still friends on and off the pitch.

Brian always found a way to get the best out of his offensive players, even if it sometimes meant playing

Walshy out of position. Sometimes, I would play alongside Quinny and Walshy would be out to one side.

If we played with three strikers, which is something Brian really liked doing at Manchester City, Walshy would be working everywhere behind me and Niall. Alongside Niall, I would be the mobile one. I didn't mind that, I was a good athlete, I could run all day.

I was injured for the 5-2 win over Tottenham. I scored 23 goals in that season – 1994/95 – and I missed eight games after picking up an ankle injury against Norwich. That was the first and only time that my parents came over to watch me because Jurgen Klinsmann was playing for Tottenham at that time. I was sitting in the stands with them.

After that game I was thinking to myself, that it would be difficult to win my place back.

However, Brian brought me on in the next game, against Wimbledon and I scored again, almost immediately and, afterwards, Brian said to me: 'Don't worry, you will play. Somehow I will get you in the team.'

It was a dressing room full of strong, experienced people like Keith Curle, Niall Quinn, Tony Coton. Good people. My English was improving but sometimes I didn't understand what was going on. Maybe that was sometimes good. The coaching staff always tried to be positive. Mossy was the funny one, Brian was a leader, Tony Coton was a very strong person – you had a good mix.

There is one day I will never forget. 7 May 1994. It was the last game of the season, at Sheffield Wednesday, and Michel Vonk came over to me during the game and said: 'The fans are singing your name.' I told him it could not be true because in Germany nobody ever sings a player's name but it was. It was on that day that I felt Manchester City was my home.

There was a very good feeling going into my second full season at Manchester City in 1994/95. Pre-season was good – I met my wife on a pre-season tour of Norway. But I started with a red card against Arsenal. After that I was so down. Brian came over and told me not to worry. He kicked my arse a little bit and told me I could play in the next game because the red card only kicks in after two weeks. We played at home to West Ham and I scored again.

Brian got the sack after one of the best games we played. We beat Blackburn, 3-2, at Ewood Park in the season where they finished as champions. All the pre-match discussion was about how many Blackburn would score. It was a rainy night and we played with Quinny, Walshy and myself up front. We surprised them, we attacked so completely.

After the game Brian told us that he would not be here next season. It was hard to take, especially for me. I had really enjoyed my football for the first 18 months in Manchester and Brian had been a big part of that.

He had signed me, he believed in me and he kept faith with me. As a foreigner, it would have been very easy to have dropped me when Quinny came back. I owe him a lot for that.

Terrier

(Games 1,122–1,241)

WHEN you are an out-of-work football manager there is always one thing that hits you. There are only 92 jobs.

Manchester City was to be the only Premier League club I was involved with until I returned with Hull as Phil Brown's assistant 12 years later. Perhaps there could have been more.

I felt I had done well at Maine Road. The fans had liked the style of football, there had been some spectacular, stand-out results; the 5-2 win over Tottenham, the back-to-back victories against Liverpool and Blackburn. With more consistency, City might have been a real force. I thought I deserved another shot at the Premier League but with jobs so limited in the professional game do you stick or do you twist?

You can wait but, if you are out of football for any length of time, you are soon forgotten. Suddenly and without quite knowing why, you become an ex-manager.

David Pleat, who had been on his second stint as a manager at Luton, had left to take over at Sheffield Wednesday and I was invited down to Kenilworth Road for what turned out to be a chat with the chairman's son rather than a formal interview. I was not offered the job, which went to Terry Westley, who lasted four months. Luton were relegated to the old Third Division in last place.

I was then invited to Bolton, who had just won promotion to the Premier League and played Liverpool in the League Cup Final. Bruce Rioch had left Burnden Park to become manager of Arsenal.

It was an attractive prospect and Bolton would be moving to the Reebok Stadium the following year but I was asked if I would be happy working under Colin Todd. I had nothing against Colin but, after two years managing in the Premier League, I didn't want to be anyone's number two. Bolton, like Luton, would finish bottom of the table.

Derby was now another prospect. In 1995 they had been mid-table in what would now be the Championship and were preparing for their final season at the Baseball Ground.

I was interviewed by the chairman, Lionel Pickering, who remembered a televised game between Oxford and Derby when I had left three players up in attack when we were defending a corner. He thought these were the kind of aggressive tactics Derby would be interested in.

The job went to my former neighbour in Woodstock, Jim Smith, who did rather well for Derby County. In his first season, he promoted them to the Premier League, oversaw the move to Pride Park and kept them in the top flight for five consecutive seasons.

I had been introduced to Huddersfield through Trevor Cherry whom I had met during the World Cup in the United States.

Trevor had been born in Huddersfield and had played for them for seven years until he was signed by Leeds in 1972. He still had a lot of connections in the boardroom at Huddersfield, who were suddenly and unexpectedly having to look for a new manager.

They had just won promotion to what would now be the Championship after beating Bristol Rovers in the play-off final but Neil Warnock had resigned following a contractual dispute and Huddersfield were searching for a replacement.

Huddersfield were a good club; they were on an upward curve and had moved into a spectacular new stadium. The only problem I could see from a manager's point of view was that the position of chairman was rotated among the directors. The club lacked a key figure with whom you could form a relationship, which was important when you wanted to do transfers quickly.

In Huddersfield's promotion season, Andy Booth had scored 26 goals. He was a fabulous header of the ball, the epitome of an English centre-forward and was only 21 when I arrived at the McAlpine Stadium.

My big idea was to pair Andy with Marcus Stewart, who had been part of the Bristol Rovers side Huddersfield had beaten in the play-off final at Wembley. The two would have been as good as any pairing in the Championship. Booth was strong and brave and Marcus Stewart was technically outstanding. He scored a complete hat-trick against Wrexham in the League Cup, one goal with the left foot, one with the right – and a header.

Dennis Booth had worked with Marcus at Bristol Rovers and I'd been following him when I was at Manchester City. On Valentine's Day 1995 I'd driven down to Brighton in the kind of pouring rain that I thought might see the game called off to watch him play at the Goldstone Ground. He scored the most fabulous goal. He danced past the centre-half, dummied the keeper to put him on his backside and walked round him to put the ball into the empty net. I thought that would do for me and went straight to my car for the journey north.

Andy Booth and Stewart never played together because in the summer of 1996 we received an offer of £2.7m for Andy from David Pleat at Sheffield Wednesday. It was the kind of money no director at Huddersfield Town could have turned down.

The deal very nearly collapsed. Booth always had problems with his knees and, when he got to Hillsborough, they showed up on the medical but David was so keen on the transfer that he pushed it through. He returned to Huddersfield five years later for £200,000.

Huddersfield started well. We won our first four home games and pushed hard near the top of the division. It was the FA Cup, or rather our elimination from the FA Cup, that was the key to our season. The early rounds had seen us overcome Blackpool and Peterborough before drawing Wimbledon, who were managed by Joe Kinnear, in the fifth round.

Huddersfield were leading 2-1 with time running out. Iain Dunn, who Neil Warnock had signed from Goole, had the ball deep in the Wimbledon half and all he had to do was keep it by the corner flag or hoof it out of play and the referee would have blown for full time.

Instead, he tried a cross, Dave Beasant caught it, booted it upfield, Wimbledon won a corner and scored from it. The full-time whistle went almost the moment the ball struck the net. We lost the replay at Selhurst Park, 3-1.

That defeat sparked a downward spiral that cost Huddersfield their chance of a second successive promotion. We had gone into the replay in fourth place. We were ten points behind Derby, who Jim Smith had taken top of the division, but there were only three points between us and Charlton, who were second.

After our exit from the FA Cup, Huddersfield took four points from our next seven games, which culminated in a 3-2 defeat at Sunderland, who by now were breaking away at the top with Derby. Despite our run of form, Huddersfield had only slipped out of the play-off positions on goal difference. We were still contenders.

By then, I had signed Ben Thornley on loan from Manchester United. Ben had been part of the Class of '92 that was starting to transform Old Trafford. Had it not been for injuries, which in turn led to problems with alcohol, and a lack of judgement, he could have hit the heights with the rest of them.

Ben was a smashing lad, who had scored at Derby in his second game for us and followed it up with the winner against Luton. He was a fiery winger who could tackle but there were times when you wondered what he was thinking.

We had been playing well at Roker Park but Ben, who had been booked early on, was becoming increasingly irritated with the referee, Neale Barry, who with the scores level at 1-1 blew for half-time. The ball was in the air when the whistle went. Thornley caught it and then threw it at the referee, who immediately sent him off.

I could not believe what I had just seen. We actually took the lead with ten men but Michael Bridges, a teenager who would have gone on to great things had he not suffered a serious injury when at Leeds, scored twice for Sunderland late on. They were goals that absolutely killed our season.

Alex Ferguson fined Thornley for that and fined him again when he was sent off in the final match of the season against Portsmouth.

There might have been questions about Ben's judgement but there were none at all about his ability. Huddersfield tried to sign him permanently in the summer but Alex Ferguson insisted that he remain at Manchester United, where he barely played.

Ben has since written that he would have been much better off playing regular first-team football at the McAlpine Stadium than wasting away with the reserves at Old Trafford.

That was not the only dealings I had with Alex Ferguson. One Sunday morning the phone rang in my flat in Bramhall. The voice on the other end of the line was seething. Alex Ferguson wanted to know why he had been sent a letter from Huddersfield accusing Manchester United of attempting to poach one of their players.

I said: 'Before you start ranting and raving, Alex, do you want to know the full story?' I told him that a few Saturdays before one of Manchester United's scouts had approached one of our young players as he came off the pitch and tapped him up, which under football's rules is an illegal approach.

I had told our academy manager, Gerry Murphy, to send a warning letter to Manchester United. When exactly the same thing happened again – same scout, same player – we sent a letter to the FA to make a formal complaint and a copy was delivered to United. I told Fergie to check the story. The next time I saw him, I said: 'Did you check the story?' He just smiled, which was as near to an apology as you were likely to get from Alex Ferguson.

Our season faded away. After beating Millwall, 3-0, at the McAlpine in April, Huddersfield were seventh, one place from the play-offs, level on points with Ipswich, one point behind Stoke in fifth. We took one point from our final four matches.

We finished eighth, which was pretty good for a newly promoted side. My brief in June had been simply to keep the club in the division.

Eighth place in the old Second Division was Huddersfield's best finish since they were relegated from the top flight in 1972 and they would not finish higher until 2017 when they went up to the Premier League under David Wagner. However, at the time it felt like a disappointment.

Then, the McAlpine Stadium only had three stands – the North Stand was not completed until 1998. There was just empty space behind one of the goals and sometimes that would affect the atmosphere, although the players never complained.

With its curved roofs, it was a beautifully designed stadium which we shared with the town's rugby league team, the Huddersfield Giants, who had gone into administration. By the time the stadium was finished off in 1998 the Giants were back in the Super League.

Because of the need to share the stadium with rugby we played on a Desso pitch which has polypropylene fibres mixed in with natural grass. The footballers found it hard to adapt because it could be rock hard. You could not wear studs on it and sometimes the players found themselves slipping all over the place.

Those players who had been part of the promotion squad also had to learn a new system because I was keen for

Huddersfield to be a much more fluid and attacking side than they had been under Neil Warnock.

If the stadium was spectacular, the fans were good and the pitch was strange, Huddersfield's training ground was distinctly shabby. They were based at Storthes Hall, a Georgian mansion which had been used as a psychiatric hospital until 1992.

To get to the pitches you had to walk along the canal, over the lock and up the hill where you found a playing surface that was often poor. It was not the kind of place where you wanted to take a potential new signing when you were trying to impress him about the kind of club he would be joining.

There was no canteen but there was a couple, Jean and Brian, who used to do the players' laundry and would make sandwiches for them. The bacon and egg rolls were particular favourites.

The sale of Andy Booth to Sheffield Wednesday in the summer of 1996 meant there was money to spend. I did the deal with Bristol Rovers for Marcus Stewart and paired him with Andy Payton, who had broken through as a centre-forward at Hull when I was manager and was now with Barnsley. That deal cost £325,000.

The £500,000 I spent on Andy Morrison bought Huddersfield a magnificent centre-half who could also play in midfield. Andy might have seemed a big, hulking lad but he was good with the ball at his feet and he was obvious captaincy material.

He was an old-fashioned leader who could grab people by the throat if it was necessary to make his point in the dressing room. I recognised something of myself in Andy. Like me, he trained like he played and, if we were having an eight v eight, he would want to win it.

Marcus Stewart was completely different, a laid-back West Country boy, whose approach reminded me of Mark Lawrenson, who was one of the least committed trainers I have ever come across but who could simply switch his talent on when Saturday afternoon came around. I could never be like that.

Managers do have a tendency to entrust the captaincy to people with similar traits to themselves. At Brighton, Alan Mullery told me that he saw something of himself when he watched me play and that is why he made me his captain.

I always liked signing players with a bit of flair, even if they were full-backs, like Steve Jenkins, who we brought in from Swansea. Steve went on to play for Wales and he loved pushing forward. The corollary to that is that you need players like Andy Morrison to underpin everything just as Brighton and Luton needed someone like Steve Foster.

Those signings should have provided Huddersfield with a platform for another push at promotion to the Premier League. We started off well. Morrison scored on his debut against Charlton, Stewie scored that fabulous hat-trick against Wrexham in the League Cup. We drew 1-1 with Crystal Palace and then beat Ipswich at Portman Road. Then injuries began weighing us down.

In our fifth game, at home to Tranmere, Andy Morrison went up for a header and felt a sharp pain in his knee and five days later was having an operation. Morrison came back for my return to Maine Road in November, which saw us get the better of a goalless draw with Manchester City. His knee swelled up again. Scans showed Andy needed another operation which put him out for another three months.

We lost Marcus Stewart, who suffered a strange injury around his ankle which we never succeeded in diagnosing properly.

Lee Makel, who had failed to break into the midfield Kenny Dalglish had built at Blackburn but who had done very well for me, was also out injured.

I had paired Lee with Darren Bullock, who had come to Huddersfield from non-league football at Malvern and Nuneaton. They were a very good pairing. Bully was a hard, physical character who would tackle anybody while Lee was a slightly built technician.

The loss of Makel, Morrison and Stewart meant we were deprived of almost £2m worth of footballers. A club like Huddersfield could not afford those kinds of losses. It was, suddenly, a team without a backbone.

On 8 October we beat Birmingham, 3-0, to go seventh. On 7 December we beat Norwich, 2-0. In between, we won one match in two months. Huddersfield were never in danger of going down but we finished 20th, two positions off a relegation place.

I have always been a bad loser. My marriage had broken up while I was at Huddersfield and I was living in a flat in Bramhall in Cheshire. I tried not to take the defeats home with me. For one thing, it was not fair on my kids. After a defeat, I would not go out on a Saturday night, not because I was afraid of meeting any fans but because I would not be good company.

If I had something to say to the players, I would wait until the Monday morning and the team meeting. Nowadays it is much more technical with DVDs that can break the game down into five-minute segments and where every player's every move is analysed.

When my third season at Huddersfield opened, it was essential to start well. I had brought in Tony Book, who had been controversially sacked by Francis Lee at Manchester City, to offer his advice and experience and do some scouting because the scouting system at Huddersfield was virtually non-existent.

However, by the time we played Nottingham Forest in early October, we were bottom of the table without a win in eight games.

Forest had been relegated from the Premier League in 1997 but with Pierre van Hooijdonk spearheading their attack they were top of the Championship. The game was on a Friday night, selected by *Sky Sports* for live television coverage. Morrison and Stewart played but I had few of my first-choice players available.

Our goalkeeper, Steve Francis, was out of action and against the league leaders, who had Dean Saunders and Kevin Campbell supporting van Hooijdonk in attack, we had Derek O'Connor, a teenager we had signed from Crumlin United in Ireland.

He did his best and was not remotely responsible for the 2-0 defeat we suffered but, elsewhere, I had to field footballers who, deep down, I knew were not good enough. That is an awful feeling.

I was sacked on the Monday morning. They wanted rid of me and my backroom team, although they wanted to keep Tony Book. It was an offer Tony refused. He told the club he had come in for me and would be going with me. Tony had a sense of honour about him. He was a gentleman.

Andy Morrison (Huddersfield Town (1996–1998)

I met Brian when I was transferred to Huddersfield from Blackpool, where we had somehow lost a play-off semi-final at home to Bradford after winning the first leg 2-0 at Valley Parade. It meant Sam Allardyce was sacked the next morning.

I had a phone call saying that they had received a bid from Huddersfield. Blackpool had agreed a fee of £500,000 and now it was up to me to speak to the club.

I rang Sam who advised me to leave. Huddersfield had a wonderful stadium and it was filled by wonderful people.

It seems strange for me to say this because I am not usually the kind of person who is intimidated but Brian did have an aura about him. He had powerful, piercing eyes and I realised very quickly that he would be very demanding.

He was a man with very high standards and was a ferocious competitor, especially in the five-a-sides. I am a manager now (with Connah's Quay) and I am the same. If you are a fierce competitor as a player, you will be exactly the same as a manager. When we had training games, I realised what a good player he had been. He would sit at the back and play the sweeper role.

Brian had a very good backroom team. David Moss was more of a coach while Dennis Booth was an incredible character, keeping the place buzzing with jokes.

He made me captain straight away which was a surprise. Lee Sinnott had been Huddersfield's skipper but he was coming towards the end of his career and Brian sussed very quickly that I was not the kind of person who could come into a changing room and not have an opinion.

When I wrote my autobiography, I said that I'd let him down. In my extra-curricular activities I did. I was 24 or 25 and rather too fond of the drink. There were a few of us in that Huddersfield team, like Darren Bullock and Marcus Stewart, who liked a drink when we were staying in a hotel.

On the pitch, I don't think I let Brian down and I don't think he would have come across many who trained or played harder than I did. I scored on my debut, against Charlton, but I was injured early on in his first season, which is the one where we might have gone up. It was the same knee injury that ultimately finished me and for the rest of my career I would try to patch that injury over but I was seldom properly fit.

At the training ground, we had a lovely lady called Jean, who did the kit and would make us beautiful bacon sandwiches. There were three of us out of the team with injuries, trying to get our fitness back sitting in the wash room eating bacon sarnies when Brian walked in, looking for his training top. He wasn't exactly happy we were eating while supposedly trying to lose weight.

Sam Collins, who was one of those injured and trying to get back to full fitness, heard Brian and came into the wash room to say he wouldn't be having the egg and bacon sandwich he had just ordered.

I told Sam I couldn't let it go to waste and was tucking into my second sandwich of the morning when the door burst open and the gaffer was shouting: 'I want all you fuckers weighed first thing in the morning.'

He turned to me and I had ketchup dribbling down my chin with an egg and bacon sandwich in my hand. He looked at me as if he could not believe what he was seeing. When I was weighed the next day, I was found to be 13 pounds overweight. Brian fined me £20 per pound until I got rid of it.

Wandering Seagull

(Games 1,242–1,286)

WHEN I left Brighton, they were a top-flight club, playing at a packed Goldstone Ground. When I returned 17 years later, they were fighting to avoid relegation from the Football League, the Goldstone Ground was being turned into a retail park, a home for B&Q rather than football, and the team was playing its home games 75 miles away in Gillingham.

In 1995 Brighton had finished 16th in what would be the old Third Division and their fans discovered the Goldstone Ground was to be sold and they would be ground-sharing with Portsmouth.

For the next two years, the club was in turmoil. There were demonstrations against the chairman, Bill Archer, they were relegated once and only survived falling out of the Football League by drawing with Hereford on the final afternoon of the season. In the middle of all this, the ground-share at Fratton Park had fallen through and they would now be playing their home fixtures at Gillingham. It took about one-and-a-half hours to drive there via three motorways. If you wanted to go by train, you had to take one north to London and then another in the opposite direction to Kent.

Just about the only thing that had not changed was that the club was still passionately supported. In 1978, when the Seagull Special was carrying fans across the country, the average attendance at the Goldstone Ground was more than 25,000. By 1995, it had fallen to 7,500. That may not sound much compared to what Brighton had been and what they are today but it was still the third-highest attendance in the division. Only Birmingham and Huddersfield, both of whom were promoted, attracted bigger crowds.

The club was a ridiculous mess. Around 2,300 now made the tortuous journey to Priestfield every other week, they had won one game in three months and were once more in danger of heading out of the Football League. I had no hesitation in signing up to become their next manager.

The offer came in a phone call from the Brighton chairman, Dick Knight, in February 1998. He told me they had very reluctantly decided to sack Steve Gritt, who had kept the club up the previous season, and asked if I would be interested in taking over. We arranged to meet at Mottram Hall.

Dick Knight was someone I liked enormously. He had made his money in advertising, had offices in London and drove a Porsche. From his point of view, appointing someone who had captained Brighton in the top flight would bring him some kudos and establish a rapport with fans who had just lost their ground.

There were reasons for me to say yes. Firstly, I had been out of work for four months and while Huddersfield had – unlike Manchester City – paid up my contract without any fuss, I still needed a job.

The other reason was more emotional. Ever since I had been driven down in a limousine from Selhurst Park to the Metropole Hotel for that meeting with Peter Taylor in 1976, I had loved Brighton, the town and the club.

Brighton was the place where I had my first little taste of management. When I signed for Brighton, we had rented a place in Withdean and one day I got a knock on the door and was greeted by three lads. They played for a team in the third division of the Sussex Sunday League and they wondered if I would come and coach them on a Thursday at the Withdean, which was the town's athletics stadium.

We would train in the football pitch in the middle of the stadium and, from there, we would often see Steve Ovett running around the track. If I was available on the Sunday, I would coach them when they played. We got promotion and we won a cup at The Dripping Pan in Lewes.

One day, I turned up on a Sunday and they were all in fancy-dress costumes. They had come from an all-night party. Fairly predictably, they were beaten.

I lost it with them. I sat them down and said: 'If you fucking expect me to come and watch you when you turn up with a hangover and play like that, then I'm finished with you.' They apologised and said it would not happen again and it did not.

I often think that, had Mike Bailey not asked me to find another club, I might never have left Brighton. I might have spent another three years as a player and then perhaps joined the coaching staff. Maybe I would have taken over as manager one day, though I never imagined it would be in circumstances like these.

The club was administered from an office in a block by Brighton Station. We trained at Falmer on the Brighton University pitches, which were absolutely shocking. We had to use the bottom of the field by the rugby pitches which at times could resemble a bog.

There was no structure to the club and, given what he had to work with, Dick Knight had done an amazing job simply to keep Brighton afloat. Without him they might not have survived. Dick had almost nothing to work with, although he did have good people around him.

Brighton may have been second bottom when I arrived but the plight of Doncaster Rovers meant there was a cushion between ourselves and last place.

That season Doncaster got through four managers, lost a record 34 games – the most for a professional club in England – and saw their chairman, Ken Richardson, arrested for trying to burn down one of the stands at their ground, Belle Vue, to collect on the insurance.

My first game was at home to Chester, although the concept of playing at home 75 miles away was an alien one. We won 3-2. There was another win at home to Scunthorpe, half-a-dozen draws and four defeats. Brighton finished with 35 points, 12 fewer than they had the previous season when they had stayed up on the final day at Hereford.

I told Dick Knight that, if I were to stay, there had to be some major changes. The chairman knew that had to happen, although he was slightly surprised by how big I wanted the changes to be.

'I want 18 out and 18 in,' I told him. 'The reserves are bottom of their league; the kids are bottom of their league and the first team finished one place off bottom place in the bottom league. There is something wrong with the club.'

There could be no room for sentiment. I kept only about three of the players I had inherited. I kept Jeff Minton, who had been the club's leading goalscorer – with seven. I kept the centre-forward, Richie Barker, and the goalkeeper, Mark Ormerod. The rest could go.

As my number two I had inherited Jeff Wood, who had been Steve Gritt's assistant at Brighton. He knew a lot of players and was absolutely invaluable when it came to rebuilding the team in that frantic summer of 1998.

Dick Knight had been sent a letter from a Brighton fan living in Essex, who suggested we check out a striker called Gary Hart, a forklift truck driver who was playing for Stansted Airport in the Essex Sunday League.

It was a league that Jeff, who had been a goalkeeper for Charlton, still used to turn out in. He checked Gary out and we put him in a reserve game against Arsenal, where he did very well against Steve Bould, who was returning from injury. We signed him for £1,000 and, instead of a sell-on clause, we gave Stansted a set of shirts.

Brighton never did sell Gary Hart but he went on to become a huge favourite with the fans, playing more than 370 games for the club and captaining them when they played their first game in the new stadium at Falmer. He had been a Brighton player for 13 years.

I paired Gary with Jamie Moralee, an experienced forward who had played for Millwall and was available on a free transfer from Crewe.

He went on to become Rio Ferdinand's agent and I dealt with him at Southend, where he represented Rio's brother, Anton.

Ian Culverhouse, who had been part of the Norwich side that had beaten Bayern Munich in the UEFA Cup in 1993, was another I brought to Brighton. He had been a very fine defender, who was now playing for Kingstonian. At Brighton, I played Ian as a sweeper.

At Huddersfield, I tended not to take potential signings to the rather ramshackle training ground but concentrate their minds on the wonderful new stadium.

At Brighton, I had a training ground many times worse than Storthes Hall and no stadium. However, I was dealing with free transfers, who had usually been let go by some other club.

They wanted to play football and, for all its difficulties, Brighton and Hove Albion were still a name. They also never had difficulty paying the wages, which was also a big thing when somebody was deciding whether to relocate.

There needed to be changes behind the scenes. I brought in Martin Hinshelwood, who would go on to become Brighton's director of football, as a youth-team coach. Alongside him was Dean Wilkins, who had played more than 300 games for Brighton and would manage the club.

Because of his business interests, I would tend to see Dick Knight only on the Friday before a game. My day-to-day dealings with the club in their little office by Brighton Station were with the club secretary Derek Allan and his secretary, Sally, two of the best people you could ever hope to meet.

My biggest transfer coup for Brighton involved someone who never played a competitive game for the club. Paul Holsgrove was a midfielder at Stoke but after they were relegated to the third tier, he was offered as a free transfer. His dad, John, had played for Walsall and his son Jordan plays for Reading. That summer Paul seemed to be a good fit to captain Brighton.

Alex McLeish, who was then managing Hibernian, had also been interested in Holsgrove but he had gone on holiday and Brighton had nipped in and completed the signing.

When McLeish returned from holiday, he called and offered £70,000 for Holsgrove. As chairman of a club who would soon have 'Skint' on their shirts after doing a deal with the Brighton-based record label, £70,000 seemed a lot of money to Dick Knight but I thought we could get more and turned Alex down.

Paul had played a few pre-season fixtures when McLeish came back again and we settled on £113,000, which was considerably more than my salary. I had effectively paid for myself.

It was not such good news for Paul Holsgrove. He had just sold his house in Stoke and was looking for property in Brighton. Suddenly, he had to move to Edinburgh. I met him a few months ago and Paul said the move had cost him a lot because the house he was going to buy on the south coast was now worth a fortune.

Gareth Barry's move to Aston Villa also made some much-needed money, even though he, like Paul Holsgrove, never played professionally for Brighton. Gareth grew up along the coast in Hastings and had been a trainee at Brighton but had left to join Aston Villa along with another young midfielder, Michael Standing, who went on to play for Bradford and Walsall. Brighton felt we were entitled to compensation.

Dick Knight asked me if I had any experience of tribunals. After my experience at Manchester City, I certainly did and in October 1998 I went with him to the tribunal at the headquarters of the Premier League.

Aston Villa, whose manager, John Gregory, used to play alongside me at the Goldstone Ground, argued that we were entitled to nothing because they had made him into a left-sided defender. That was where Gareth had played when he first broke into the first team at Villa Park.

Les Rogers, who had coached Barry at the Brighton centre of excellence, successfully argued that this was one of several positions where Gareth had played in our youth teams.

Villa were also trying to argue that they were taking a risk by signing him. They claimed they did not know whether Barry would make it as a Premier League footballer. I pointed out to the tribunal that there could be no risk to them because Gareth was already a Premier League first-team footballer when the tribunal convened. He had already broken through.

The Premier League ordered Aston Villa to make an immediate payment of £150,000. If Barry played for England – he made his full debut in September 2000 – Brighton would be due more than £1m.

In August, at Scarborough, Brighton won their first away game in 21 months. Between October and December, we won six out of seven league fixtures.

The first of those victories was at Barnet with the winning goal scored by a big Nigerian centre-half called Emeka Ifejiagwa, whom I had spotted playing for Charlton Reserves.

He was already a Nigeria international but couldn't get a game for Alan Curbishley's first team so I arranged a loan deal. Emeka's second game produced a 3-2 win over Hartlepool.

It was too good to last. I was contacted by the Home Office who stated that Ifejiagwa did not have a permit to work in England and would have to return to Nigeria. He couldn't even go back to Charlton.

He turned up playing for Osasuna in La Liga and for Wolfsburg in the Bundesliga and made a dozen appearances for Nigeria, who were then Olympic champions. At the level Brighton found themselves in, he would have been formidable.

On Boxing Day, we were at home – if you can describe Gillingham as home – to Brentford, whose chairman, Ron Noades, has just appointed himself as manager.

As a player and a manager, I had always insisted that we should train on Christmas Day if we were playing the following afternoon. Football was not our hobby; it was our livelihood.

However, because of the situation Brighton were in, I thought this might be an exception. Our goalkeeper, Mark Ormerod, lived in Southampton, and quite a few players lived in or around London. In 1998, Brighton and Hove Albion did not have that many players who lived in Brighton.

I told them they could have Christmas Day off but I wanted them at Priestfield an hour and a half before the game started – and this one was an early kick-off. I warned them not to be late.

My Christmas had been spent with Val, who was to become my second wife, in our apartment in Bramhall and I set off at four on Boxing Day morning. It was the most bizarre journey. There was not another car on the road. I flew down.

We beat Brentford, 3-1, with goals from Rod Thomas, Jeff Minton and Andy Arnott. I was having a drink with Dick

Knight and Ron Noades, who asked how I had prepared the team. I told Noades I had given them Christmas Day off and we had just met at the ground.

He told me Brentford, who were second in the table, had trained on Christmas Day, travelled down to Gillingham overnight, stayed in a hotel and then been completely outplayed. There was no rhyme nor reason to the result.

In mid-January we were a point off a play-off place. It was then, while watching a game at Wycombe, that I received a phone call from Port Vale. They were getting rid of John Rudge.

That was big news. John had been Port Vale's manager for 16 years. Two years before, he had taken Port Vale to their best post-war finish, eighth in the old Second Division.

They had started to finish above Stoke regularly, which would have been unheard of when I was playing at Vale Park in the 1970s. However, they were now second bottom of what would now be the Championship and the chairman, Bill Bell, had decided to make the change.

The decision I faced was the hardest I have ever had to take. I loved Brighton but the lack of any structure at the club and the fact we were playing our home matches at Gillingham was draining. You would be driving up the M23, along the M25 and down the M2 just to play a home game. It was crazy – and yet 3,000–4,000 fans did it every other week.

Port Vale's biggest pull was not that they were two divisions above Brighton but that the Potteries was considerably nearer my family than the south coast of England.

I was divorced. The twins, who were just starting secondary school, still lived with Denise and I thought it was important to be near them.

During the week, I was living in the Courtlands Hotel in Hove, which was where visiting teams stayed when they played Sussex at the County Ground. I had stayed at the Courtlands when I first joined Brighton in 1976 and the team would have its pre-match lunch there.

I would leave Bramhall very early on a Monday morning and drive the five hours to Brighton and return on the Saturday night.

I had just taken delivery of a new car from the Mercedes garage in Brighton, a beautiful 2.2 E Class and had set off for the south coast very early one March morning. I was driving on the bypass near Alderley Edge, slowing down for the roundabout, doing about 50mph when it felt as if I had struck a brick wall.

There had been flash floods overnight and that, coupled with some subsidence, had left a pool of water three feet deep which I had not seen. The Mercedes crashed into it, the lights went out, the electrics failed and I was stuck in the water. When I opened the door, the interior of the car began to flood.

I managed to make my way to the central reservation and phone the police. It was too deep for them to be able to do anything and a tow-truck had to be called out.

What made it worse was this was transfer deadline day. There were three or four players due in. I had to get to

Brighton so I phoned Val and said: 'I am terribly sorry but I need your car.'

She came out to the lay-by where I had been stranded, handed over her Vauxhall Corsa and while she stayed with my car while it was towed to the Mercedes garage in Macclesfield, I drove the Corsa south.

The Mercedes was a complete write-off. I had phoned the club to tell them what had happened and, when I arrived in my office, someone had put a pair of flippers on my desk.

Dick Knight knew my situation and knew the pull that Port Vale would have. Port Vale had agreed to pay Brighton a year of my salary, which was about £80,000, so they would be receiving some financial compensation but Dick would rather not have taken the money.

He tried his very best to persuade me to stay, pointing out that Brighton might be able to start playing at the Withdean athletics ground next season and they could start to rebuild in the town itself.

He was right – Brighton moved to the Withdean, which had a capacity of 8,800 the following season – but at the time I could not envisage it. I could not see how Brighton were going to move forward and, after so long away, I felt I owed it to my children to be near them. Football had been the driving force in my life and perhaps this was the one time where I put my family first.

Valiant Again

(Games 1,287–1,547)

I WAS coming back to where my professional football career had begun nearly 30 years before. I was also coming back into a hornets' nest.

John Rudge could claim to be the greatest manager in Port Vale's history. He had been appointed three years before Alex Ferguson had taken over at Manchester United and in terms of league position had made Port Vale the leading club in the Potteries. They were in the Championship, a division above Stoke.

However, Port Vale were going down. They had lost 12 of their last 14 games. They were second from bottom, three points from safety. They had also scored fewer goals than anyone in the division except Bury. That season the number of goals you scored would be important.

The Football League had ruled that goals scored, rather than goal difference, would separate teams that finished level on points.

There was a frostiness when I arrived. John Rudge, whom I had known a long time, thought that I had gone behind his back to get the job, that I had negotiated with the directors at Port Vale while he was still in post.

That offended me because in all my years in football it is something I have never done.

There are some football managers who, if they are out of work or looking for a move, make a point of going to a ground where another manager is in trouble. They will make sure they are seen and are available for a conversation in the directors' lounge. It is appalling behaviour and something I have never taken part in.

Some time afterwards, I met John Rudge and said to him: 'John, believe what you want to believe, but I am here to tell you that I never negotiated behind your back.'

Port Vale were also in financial difficulties because they had demolished the old Lorne Street Stand and were spending £3m on building a new stand which transformed the ground but which the club could not afford. The chairman, Bill Bell, wanted to make Vale Park a 20,000-seater stadium.

It was a great ambition, and one which I could understand, but it was unrealistic given where the club was. Port Vale had good, loyal fans but they were never going to fill a 20,000-seater stadium.

When Vale Park opened in 1950, its capacity had been 40,000. In only one season did Port Vale attract even half that – in 1954/55 when they had won promotion to the old

Second Division after reaching the semi-finals of the FA Cup. The last year in which gates were averaging 10,000 was 1964.

The stand was being built when I arrived, which meant the directors' room was in a Portakabin.

Bill Bell was an old-fashioned chairman. His background was in car dealerships and he knew my brother, John, better than he knew me because John had the King Ford franchise in Stoke. His daughter, Linda, and his son-in-law, Andy Belfield, were also on the board.

When I came into a club, I was never the sort that began by laying into the players, accusing them of getting my predecessor the sack and threatening them. I thought these were men I would need and it would be in everyone's interests to keep them onside.

At Vale Park there would have been players who would have known only Rudge's management and you wonder how they will respond to your voice. My experience is that they get on and play. Martin Foyle, whom I had managed at Oxford, had spent seven years being managed by John and he played no differently for me.

Because the club was in such freefall, I decided I had to make some changes immediately. I knew very few of the younger players so I organised a practice match as soon as I could. I could then look at the hand I'd been dealt.

Anthony Gardner seemed excellent. He was born in Staffordshire, he was just 18, he was 6ft 5in tall, lightning-quick and the following year we would sell him to Tottenham for £1m. I wanted him in the team as part of a back five to shore up the defence and make Port Vale harder to beat.

I asked one of the backroom staff I had inherited from John Rudge why Gardner hadn't been in the first team.

'He cost us a goal at Wolves a few weeks back and he hasn't played since.'

'Judging from the league table, he isn't the only one who's costing goals.'

Gardner, bluntly, looked too good for a club that was practically bottom of the division to do without.

We kept a clean sheet – the first time Port Vale had managed that in nearly two months – in my first game as manager. It was a 2-0 victory over Huddersfield. Martin Foyle, one of Port Vale's great centre-forwards, scored both goals.

That season he would score one more, against Barnsley – which earned us another three points.

Martin was 35 and he was not the only one in his thirties. The squad had been allowed to grow old together and I joked to the chairman I had inherited Dad's Army.

Experience was a double-edged sword. If Port Vale were to survive, then the experienced players like Martin Foyle, Ian Bogie and Neil Aspin were the likeliest men to dig us out of the hole.

At the same time, they would very obviously soon have to be replaced and for a club heading for the financial rocks like Port Vale, they were the men on the biggest money.

Managing Brighton at home, at Gillingham.

HORTON'S HOTLINE PROVES A BIG SPUR

HEYDAY: David Pleat while with Luton

ALBION boss Brian Horton has revealed his close relationship with David Pleat.

His Sunday morning ritual is a telephone chat with Tottenham's respected Director of Football about players and what is happening in the game.

The pair have been friends ever since Pleat signed Horton for Luton from the Seagulls in August 1981.

"He made me captain and I had a great relationship with him," Horton said.

"The only medal I ever won was in my first year at Luton, when we won the Second Division.

"He helped me get my first job in management at Hull and we still speak every Sunday morning.

"The conversation is always totally about football, not how your golf handicap is or anything like that.

"When I was at Manchester City and he was at Luton we would talk about players who might help each other.

Knowledge

"Now that he's at Tottenham and I'm at Brighton we talk a lot about reserve players.

"I've learnt a lot from David and I just appreciate his knowledge.

"He's produced some good sides in his day and he's a shrewd judge.

"He's totally different to Alan Mullery. He didn't go mad after games but would wait until the Monday.

"I can't do that, I'm too volatile. Like Alan though he always wanted us to play.

"I remember us losing 6-0 at Liverpool once when they were in their prime.

"He came in and said well done played some good stuff."

A touch of Pleat-type psychology served Horton well over the festive period.

He gave the players a surprise break from Christmas Day training and they rewarded him with maximum points against Brentford and Peterborough.

Wherever I have managed I have always been able to call on David Pleat for advice.

CENTRE STAGE: Mark Lawrenson and Brian Horton answer questions last night

Look who's in town

ALBION legend Mark Lawrenson gave the cash-strapped Seagulls a helping hand last night by offering his services free of charge for a fans forum.

He flew down from his Newcastle home to sit alongside his old buddy Brian Horton on the panel at Hove dog stadium.

The pair reminisced about the good old days and answered questions about Albion in the present and future from a 100-strong audience.

Chairman Dick Knight was sidelined by illness, so Director Martin Perry was drafted in as a late substitute.

Raising money was always a priority at Brighton. Mark Lawrenson helps out at a fans' forum.

Leaving Brighton was the hardest footballing decision I have had to take.

A major problem I faced when returning to Port Vale in January 1999 was that I was replacing the club's greatest manager, John Rudge.

Celebrating victory in a Potteries derby in March 2001.

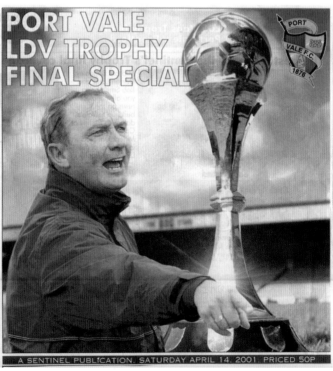

Reaching for the LDV Vans Trophy. It was only the second piece of significant silverware Port Vale would win.

My wedding to Val in October 2002 provided a rare break in the football season.

Manager of the Month, August 2003.

REPORT BY
PAUL HINCE

Nobby, the boss City ditched, is game's Red Adair

THERE'S a branch of journalism which remains a mystery even to those of us who have worked in the industry for more years than we care to remember.

It's the shadowy bunch who beaver away in their own little world under the general title of 'headline writer'.

To be fair, this breed apart has given us some fun down the years. Whoever thought up "Freddie Starr Ate My Hamster" is a genius in my book.

Naturally, sports journalism has a sprinkling of these creatures who can destroy a career with a few viciously-funny words.

Remember the classic "Turnip" headline which preceded Graham Taylor's dismissal as England manager? You can bet your life Graham hasn't forgotten.

Cutting

But few sporting headlines from the past dozen years have been quite as cutting as that in one national paper in 1993-94. It asked: "Brian Who?" and fronted the story of City's decision to appoint Brian Horton as successor to Peter Reid.

It carried an element of truth. Horton was not the big name Blues fans expected when Reid was shown the door four games into the season.

But it was insulting, nonetheless. Not one person in the soccer industry would have asked "Brian Who?"

Inside the game, few men enjoyed the respect of their peers more than Horton, who was known in dressing-rooms from Sunderland to Southampton simply as "Nobby".

As a player with clubs like Luton and Brighton, Nobby Horton acquired a reputation as a midfielder it was best not to take liberties with.

He may not have been blessed with the silky skills of a Glenn Hoddle but he compensated with a ferocious determination and a hatred of losing. He was a born leader. The captain of every club he played for. His manager's voice on the field and obvious management material when he hung up his boots.

His chance came when he stepped into the hot seat at Hull City.

Raw as he was, Horton breathed new life into one of soccer's sleeping giants with crowds of 20,000 packing Boothferry Park. He certainly impressed his employers, who co-opted him on to the board as the first director-manager in English soccer. Not bad going for a former midfield brusier in his first job on the other side of the soccer fence.

A silly tiff with his chairman – which both men later regretted –led to Horton packing his bags and accepting an invitation from Mark Lawrenson to join Oxford as assistant manager.

What the new team at the Manor Ground had no way of knowing, of course, was that Oxford was about to become a play-thing for publishing tycoon Robert Maxwell.

When 'Captain Bob' added a football club to his possessions, Lawrenson – displaying much more sense than his assistant - baled out.

Nobby was left holding the baby. And Oxford turned out to be one baby that not even a mother could love. And logic suggests that when the Maxwell empire collapsed, Oxford United should have gone down with it.

But somehow Horton kept the little club afloat. Any player who could command a transfer fee was sold to meet running costs.

Relegation looked certain, but it didn't happen under Nobby's stewardship - as near to a miracle as you are likely to encounter.

This then, was the "Brian Who?" of the newspaper headlines when Manchester City brought him to Maine Road back in 1993.

He was now recognised as a "fire-fighter", but if he thought he wouldn't need his asbestos suit at City, he was soon to discover how wrong he was.

Horton walked into more of a war-zone than a club. A bitter power struggle was under way between chairman Peter Swales and would-be successor Francis Lee.

For months, soccer took second place to events off the pitch.

Privately Horton confessed that City were unmanageable.

Numbered

Publicly he never complained as he set about returning the Blues to their former glories. How much he would have achieved we will never know. His days were numbered from the moment Lee won his takeover battle.

Horton secured the services of some of the most popular players in City's recent history in Paul Walsh, Uwe Rosler and the hyper-active, eccentric winger Peter Beagrie. The fans responded to Horton's no-nonsense style and the feast of attacking football his team displayed in 1994-95.

But a slump during the second half of that campaign took the Blues close to the relegation zone.

Opinion among the faithful was that, given time, the Blues could emerge for another Premiership force. But Nobby was never given that time. At the end of that season, tired of speculation about his future, he gave Lee a "back-me or sack-me" ultimatum.

The answer wasn't the one he wanted. But City fans to this day have not forgotten the job Horton did at Maine Road.

No ex-boss is in such demand as Horton to appear at branch meetings of City Supporters' Association. One branch even pleaded with him to become their president but reluctantly, he said no. And with good reason. He was, at the time, manager at Port Vale!

Since leaving Maine Road, Horton has strengthened his reputation as soccer's 'Red Adair'.

Brighton's existence in the League was under serious threat. No ground, no money and a threadbare playing staff. Right up Nobby's street.

Put out the fire and save them from the Conference? Of course he did.

Port Vale recruited him. After years in the doldrums, Vale under Horton's stewardship looked down on all their rivals from the top of the Third Division earlier this season.

The team was assembled by Horton for just £15,000.

But with Vale still involved in the promotion race, Horton and his employers parted company, as it became clear that further financial cut-backs were necessary.

Those of us who have monitored Nobby's career were in no way surprised when he received an SOS from Macclesfield.

Club in crisis. Send for "Nobby". Crisis solved. And so it was.

A few weeks ago I wouldn't have gambled on Macc preserving their League status. Now they are safe for another season and probably longer if they have the sense to secure Nobby's services permanently.

How has Horton achieved so much with so little? I have no idea. But wouldn't it be wonderful if just once before he calls it a day, he landed a job at a major club with REAL money? No, forget that. It's so long since Nobby had a transfer kitty he wouldn't know what to do with it.

■ TRUE BLUE... Horton during his spell at Manchester City

■ SILVER SALVO... Horton lifts the LDV Vans Trophy in 2001

After I left Manchester City, the budgets became smaller but the sense of commitment remained the same.

Former Vale boss takes over at struggling Macclesfield

Horton: It's good to be back in manager's role

by Michael Baggaley

FORMER Port Vale manager Brian Horton says his love of the cut and thrust of management prompted his decision to accept the offer to take charge at Macclesfield Town.

The Third Division strugglers have appointed the 55-year-old as a consultant and manager to help them beat the drop into the Conference.

Horton has been appointed until the end of the season, after which he will hold talks with the Macclesfield board to determine his future.

His decision to take the job will save Vale an undisclosed sum under the terms of the deal the club reached with Horton when they parted by mutual consent on February 5.

Horton says he has been itching to get back into the game since leaving Vale Park after five years.

He added: "I could have sat back and done nothing because of my con- tract with Port Vale, but I chose not to because I have missed management, which you do after 20 years. I have missed Port Vale after a long association with the club.

"I have always wanted to get back into the game. It's not as though I said I'd had enough when I left Vale."

Horton will link up with his former Vale players Tommy Widdrington and Matt Carragher at Moss Rose, but he will have no opportunity to ease into the job as the Silkmen lie second from bottom of Division Three, three points from safety.

Horton added: "They are all tough challenges to be truthful. It is not often you get a job when things are going well. Martin Foyle came in at Vale when we were close to the play- offs, but it is not often you get that. I joined Brighton when they were second from bottom before taking them up the table and Manchester City were towards the bottom when I went there. I also kept Vale up in my first season there.

"I am looking forward to this. I have missed the training and banter with the players, which is a big part of the game. I hadn't applied for any jobs, but Macclesfield is just down the road and I know most of the players."

Macclesfield approached Horton on Wednesday, having already demoted John Askey to assistant-manager.

Horton wants Askey to stay on and says he will not be making any changes to staff.

Back in action: Brian Horton

I was advised not to go to Macclesfield in March 2004 to try to preserve their Football League status. I am glad I accepted the challenge.

Express Sport

In association with Boddingtons

PART OF MANCHESTER SINCE 1778

Welchy targets a first team return

■ Turn to page 100

■ Sportsdesk: 0161 475 4878   ■ E-mail: maccsport@gmwn.co.uk   ■ Fax: 01625 618853   ■ Website: www.macclesfield-express.co.uk

1,000 NOT OUT!

Horton celebrates a milestone mark

by Marc Iles

LINE-UP - Horton's days at Maine Road with City legend Tony Book

MACC BOUND - Horton and former Silkmen boss Dave Moss

BRIAN HORTON is set to crack the 1,000-game mark as a manager when the Silkmen take on Mansfield Town at Moss Rose next Tuesday night.

The Macc Town boss joins elite company in the likes of Alex Ferguson, Dario Gradi, Joe Royle and Dave Bassett in having reached four figures - but the man himself believes few others will reach the milestone in today's football-obsessed society.

"This will be my 21st season in football management and I suppose it is an achievement considering the average for a manager at his first club these days is something like 13 months.

"The media have had a lot to do with it. Football is on SKY all the time and in the papers all the time so your performance is always under scrutiny.

"The media obviously have a job to do, but if you're not successful you have them and the fans calling for your head.

"I have been lucky to have a few spells of nearly five years at clubs, and I think that must show I can do the job."

Horton played over 700 league games as a professional after starting at his home-town club Hednesford Town, enjoying distinguished spells at Port Vale, Brighton, Luton Town, Hull City and Oxford.

"It was about the age of 27 and 28 I started thinking about the long term and taking my coaching badges," Horton told Express Sport.

"I had always been the PFA representative or the captain at the clubs I was at, so I suppose you could say I knew I wanted to be a manager."

Horton became player/manager at Hull, leading them to promotion in his first year before moving to Oxford alongside Mark Lawrenson. Whilst at the Manor Ground, he became the first-ever player/manager/director, and performed miracles on a small budget

before making his career-defining move to Manchester City.

Despite guiding City to safety in the top flight, he lost his job after Francis Lee took over and went immediately to Huddersfield, where he missed out on the play-offs by a whisker.

After leaving Yorkshire, Horton returned to Brighton, saving them from relegation to the conference before leaving for Port Vale and winning the LDV Vans Trophy.

He arrived at Macc with the club struggling at the foot of League Two, and transformed their fortunes before guiding them to their current position of fifth.

Horton lists players such as Richard Jobson, Jim Magilton, Paul Simpson, Andy Melville, Uwe Rosler and Paul Walsh among the best he has ever signed, but has no regrets about his time in football.

"I'm 55 now, and had a great career in football. I've met some fantastic people, I've been all over the world and seen some amazing things so I don't look back on any negatives in my footballing life."

HAPPY - It's all smiles last week after a 1-0 win against Oxford Utd

Chris Kamara

Joining the select band of those who have managed a thousand games. November 2004.

HORTON SURE IS GRAND

IT seems like more managers have left clubs than leaves have fallen from the trees this Autumn.

So I take this opportunity to celebrate the latest '1,000 match man'. The achievement of being in charge of more than 1,000 League and cup games in England is quite something.

I believe I have the definitive list (if you can come up with any others please email me suggestions to: fl@pa.press.net), which is: Alec Stock, Brian Clough, Dario Gradi, Jim Smith, Alan Buckley, Lennie Lawrence, Sir Matt Busby, Denis Smith, Graham Taylor, Joe Royle and Dave Bassett.

Marking his 20th anniversary of entering management this very year, the respected Brian Horton joins that elite list of managers. At 54, and now at Macclesfield, Brian is now one of the game's great survivors, someone who sees his only role in life as being a

football manager. He was first player-manager at Hull City from 1984, moving to Oxford in 1988 before his most high-profile appointment at Man City from August of 1993 to May of 1995.

He then had two years at Huddersfield, a year at Brighton, almost five at Port Vale, and has been at Macclesfield since March this year.

I remember well when he got the job at Maine Road, taking over from Peter Reid. It was very much a case of 'Brian who?', but he proved what a good manager he was there.

The end came, he admits, when he got involved in some of the political stuff behind the scenes and was shown the door when Frannie Lee's consortium took over.

I don't think people realised how good he was until he left and the club fell to pieces. Brian has been one of those great servants of

the game who ploughs on regardless of the fact that his abilities have not been recognised since by a big club.

He is a lifelong Wolves fan and would love nothing more to be given a chance to manage at that club, but the fans just wouldn't have it because he is not a big enough name.

When he took over at Macclesfield last season they were in danger of going down as they languished in the bottom two, but now things are very different and they are closer to the top. They are even an outside bet for promotion. Macclesfield in League One would be quite some achievement!

Brian's career has been varied with seven different clubs, but he has always produced honest teams that play good football.

His milestone of matches is a real achievement.

Read my betting tips in BETfirst - pages 24-25

Milestone: Brian Horton has joined an elite group of football managers by taking charge of more than 1,000 matches

A tribute from Chris Kamara after passing the milestone.

Fire-fighting Horton is doing one Hull of a job

TALKING SPORT

PAUL HINCE

THE old adage that behind every good man there's a good woman is not strictly true.

Up at the KC Stadium, Hull City's phenomenal start to their first Premier League campaign can be attributed to the fact that behind one good man at that club stands another one.

Tigers manager Phil Brown has received a blizzard of plaudits from all quarters for steering his team into a Champions League position.

And while Brown richly deserves those accolades, he will be the first to admit that his assistant Brian 'Nobby' Horton has played a huge part in Hull's fairytale season.

"I went for knowledge and experience when I chose Nobby as my assistant and he has supplied it in bundles," said Brown.

"Brian is a member of an elite group of managers who have selected 1,000 teams during his career. What he doesn't know about football isn't really worth knowing."

It's the oldest gag in sport, but the hugely popular Horton really has had more clubs than Jack Nicklaus.

Ironically enough, he started his managerial career at Hull before setting off on a nomadic trek up and down the country where he took charge of exotic clubs like Brighton, Oxford United, Port Vale and Macclesfield Town to name but a few.

There was a common denominator which joins all those clubs. Each was in real danger of relegation when he arrived – all were safe as houses when he left.

Even when Horton finally got the major platform he deserved as Manchester City's manager, he quickly discovered that he had another fire-fighting mission on his hands.

When he arrived at Maine Road he took over a club in chaos. A bitter takeover war was raging between chairman Peter Swales and wannabe chairman Francis Lee. As Horton himself said at the time, he had just become the manager of an unmanageable club.

The history books will tell you that Nobby achieved very little at Maine Road but sometimes the facts mask the truth.

Silverware

I reported on every City match for this newspaper during Brian's tenure and there was no doubt in my mind that with time and two or three more quality players he would have brought major silverware to Maine Road.

Chairman Lee sacked a good man when he dispensed with Horton's services and paid the price when a once great club plunged down the divisions like a stone.

Now, at last, this most likeable and capable man is showing the top flight what he is all about and it would be no surprise to me – or to Brown – if he was head-hunted again by other Premier League clubs.

"Brian has been a fantastic help to me during his time at the KC Stadium but really he's a manager rather than an assistant," admitted Brown.

"He doesn't feel his days as a number one are over and neither do I.

"I wanted him to feel that way and most certainly wouldn't stand in his way if he was offered a job he wanted. He would be an asset to any club at any level."

At Hull, for probably the first time in his managerial career, Horton is not needed as a fire-fighter, but as a coach. And his influence on the Tigers this season has been there for all to see.

If Tottenham Hotspur had appointed Brian Horton as manager instead of Juande Ramos, that famous old club wouldn't now be propping up the rest of the division and already facing the very real prospect of relegation.

In fact, it rings a bell doesn't it, Nobby? Club in crisis. Fighting job to be done. Keep your mobile handy, Brian. You might be back in the big time as a manager in your own right sooner than you think.

The start of a long relationship with Phil Brown.

ALL PART OF THE
SUCCESS STORY:
Phil Brown, far
right, with
assistant manager
Brian Horton and,
inset, from top,
first-team coach
Steve Parkin,
goalkeeping coach
Mark Prudhoe...

A reason for Hull's climb through the divisions lay in the backroom staff. First-team coach, Steve Parkin, goalkeeping coach, Mark Prudhoe, and physio, Simon Maltby.

HONORARY **TIGER**

Brian Horton's experience has proved vital back up to manager Phil Brown this season.

"THE TEAM ETHIC AND
THE TOGETHERNESS –
WHICH YOU SEE WHEN
YOU COME TO THE
TRAINING GROUND –
HAS BEEN FIRST CLASS"

Celebrating success on Humberside.

A discussion on the Wembley touchline against Bristol City as fourth official Phil Dowd looks on.

Celebrating with Phil Brown and chairman, Paul Duffen, as Hull reach the top flight for the first time in their history.

'SPIT SPAT' GOES INTO EXTRA TIME

DETERMINED: Duffen says City right to pursue justice

HULL City chairman Paul Duffen insists the club is right to pursue its spitting case against Arsenal captain Cesc Fabregas.

The Tigers are still to make an official complaint to the Football Association after claiming Fabregas spat at assistant manager Brian Horton.

They failed to meet an initial FA deadline of today, but have now been granted an extension until next Monday to make their case.

Fabregas has strongly denied the allegations, first made in television interviews after the FA Cup quarter-final tie by furious Tigers' manager Phil Brown.

And today, Duffen stressed the club remained determined to prove their case.

He said playing commitments and players being on international duty had prevented City from making their complaint

>> WE'RE IN THE RIGHT: Paul Duffen

official so far.

But he insists the club will be doing so, and that they will eventually be fully vindicated for their actions.

He told the Mail: "We applied to extend the deadline because many of the people who witnessed the incident are presently away from the club.

"It is not something we are going to drop because we still stand by exactly what we said on the night.

"The only way we may consider our stance would be if Arsenal were to come out and say something that would deflate the situation.

"When this matter has run its course everybody will find out that what Phil Brown has said is the truth."

Asked if the ongoing issue could prove a distraction in City's Premier League survival battle, Duffen said that wasn't a concern.

He said: "It won't be a distraction on the footballing side at all as it is a matter that is taking up

zero space in terms of what is going on at our club.

"It is simply a case of people making statements as to what happened."

Duffen labelled widespread criticism of Brown in the national media following the game, including high-profile Daily Mail columnist Piers Morgan, as 'disgraceful'.

But he added: "I suppose in a way it is a back-handed compliment to Hull City and the impact we have made in the Premier League that so many columnists still want to write about us."

A spokesman for the FA said: "We have now received a request from Hull for an extension of the deadline for them to provide their observations.

"Having considered the request, in the circumstances, we have decided to allow an extension until the end of business next Monday, March 30."

What do you think?
Visit www.sporthull.co.uk

The spitting incident involving Arsenal's Cesc Fabregas in March 2009 was a rare unpleasant moment in Hull's first season in the big time.

Looking determined with Paul Dickov at Doncaster.

Reunited with Brighton's 1979 promotion side.

With Alan Mullery at the Amex.

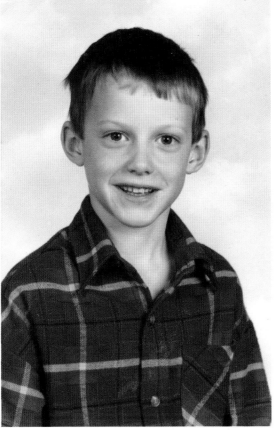

Matthew as a boy.

Lucy. Both children had to move home as my football career took me from Humberside to Oxford and then to Manchester.

Matthew and his partner Emily.

Lucy, her partner Simon and stepdaughter, Imogen.

With stepson Simon.

Brian with Val at NW Awards.

Val's granddaughter, Layla.

Brian and Val.

Transfer deadline day, 1999, was absolutely frantic. I bought in five players. Carl Griffiths, a centre-forward whom I'd brought to Manchester City, cost £100,000 from Leyton Orient. Dave Brammer, a midfielder whose father was from Burslem, was £350,000 from Wrexham. Two defenders, Tony Butler and Alex Smith, cost £180,000 between them from Blackpool and Chester. I signed Chrissy Allen on loan from Nottingham Forest until the end of the season.

Some worked and some didn't. We made a £25,000 profit on Tony Butler when we sold him to West Bromwich Albion, where he would help Gary Megson's side win promotion to the Premier League in 2002.

We sold Carl Griffiths back to Orient in December for £10,000 less than we paid for him. Chrissy Allen scored only once for us but it was the equaliser against Stockport and Port Vale would stay in the second tier of English football on goals scored.

Dave Brammer was the most expensive and the best of the five. After we had secured our status, I made him captain. He was a fine footballer who would lead us to victory in the FA Trophy Final and who went to Crewe for £150,000 more than we paid for him. He would then do very well at Stoke.

I spent £630,000 on deadline day and part-financed it by selling one of our strikers, Peter Beadle, to Notts County for £250,000. That was £50,000 less than John Rudge had paid Bristol Rovers for Beadle but we needed to raise money and he was the most saleable player that we could afford to let go.

Port Vale had 17 games remaining when I arrived. We took 22 points from those matches which over the course of a season would have been enough for a mid-table finish, just above West Bromwich Albion. Over 17 games it was enough to see Port Vale fourth bottom.

We beat some big teams – Crystal Palace and Barnsley had both been in the Premier League the season before – while a 4-3 victory over Norwich was almost doubly vital because the number of goals scored was so important.

On 1 May we beat Queens Park Rangers at home with goals from Anthony Gardner and Carl Griffiths which virtually guaranteed our survival.

Bristol City and Oxford had already been relegated to the third tier and there was one match remaining. We were fifth from bottom. Port Vale's last game was away to Bury, managed by Neil Warnock, who occupied the final relegation place.

Had goal difference been a factor rather than goals scored, they might have really fancied their chances. Port Vale had three more points than Bury but Warnock's team had a better goal difference. If they beat us at Gigg Lane, they would have been safe and we would have been down.

As it was, we had scored 45 goals and Bury had scored 34. To survive, they needed to beat us by 12 clear goals. They won, 1-0, and went down. I had fulfilled the brief I had been given but I knew the real work was still to come.

The following season would be Port Vale's sixth in what would now be the Championship and it would be the last. For the first time in my career as a player or manager which began at Vale Park in 1970, I would endure relegation. We began well with a goalless draw at Ewood Park against Blackburn, who had been relegated from the Premier League four years after winning it, but the trajectory was always downwards.

Port Vale greeted the new century with a 2-1 home defeat to Ipswich which left us fourth from bottom and in the second half of the season we won only three games – against Sheffield United, Birmingham and Portsmouth. We finished second bottom, 13 points adrift of West Brom and safety. We were relegated on Easter Monday after a 2-1 defeat to Huddersfield.

Well before relegation was confirmed, the board began asking for cuts to the wage bill.

Neil Aspin, who had been at the club for ten years, had already left. He had been given a testimonial in which Port Vale's most famous fan, Robbie Williams, played on the wing after flying back from America for the game.

Neil, who had gone to the same school as Paul Gascoigne – who didn't turn up for the testimonial – moved back to the North East to play for Darlington. Paul Musselwhite, who had kept goal for more than 300 league games, went first to Sheffield Wednesday and then to Hull.

Martin Foyle played his last season for the club and scored his final goal for us in a 2-2 draw at Charlton in November 1999. He retired at the end of the season and joined the coaching staff, initially looking after the youth team.

Robbie Williams agreed to play in Martin's testimonial in 2001 and I arranged with Joe Royle for Manchester City to come down, which doubled the usual attendance. What amazed me was that Robbie was terribly nervous. Before the game I had gone into the dressing room to see Robbie and his friend, Jonathan Wilkes – who was a very good footballer – smoking cigarettes before the game kicked off. They were very uptight about playing at Vale Park. It is astonishing when you think that Robbie would play Knebworth in front of 125,000.

Marcus Bent was sold to Sheffield United for £375,000 – which was a £75,000 profit on what we had paid Crystal Palace. As a manager, if you are told to balance the books, it is usually pretty naïve to protest when you are asked to reduce the wage bill.

Getting rid of footballers is probably the most unpleasant job a manager can have. I found it hardest letting young players or apprentices go. The older pros could usually take it and they would probably know what was coming but for a teenager to be told there was no longer a place for him at the club could be heartbreaking.

When I was managing Manchester City, I signed the release forms for a teenaged midfielder called Simon McMain, whom the club had taken from Crewe Alexandra. I always insisted to City's academy manager, Terry Farrell, that I signed the release forms because I knew the heartbreak of being released as a teenager. Many years later, I met Simon.

He was Val's son. My stepson has never held my signature on the release forms against me.

I had never forgotten how I was told I was not wanted at Walsall. Usually, if I had to let a young player go, I would tell him not to despair but to go into the world and prove me wrong.

When I was manager of Hull, I said exactly those words to Dean Windass. He did what I had done after getting out of Ray Shaw's car at Walsall bus station.

Like me, he went to work on a building site and combined it with playing non-league football at North Ferriby United. I became a top-flight footballer and so did Dean. I always tried to stress that being released did not have to be the end.

At a club like Port Vale which was struggling to stay up and struggling with its finances, you had to constantly wheel and deal. The money I was able to offer players I brought in was often around a quarter paid to the players I was having to let go.

One of my best pieces of business was for Marc Bridge-Wilkinson, who was a product of the Derby academy. He had only made one appearance for the club, although that was in a victory at Liverpool, and I offered Jim Smith money for him. It was peanuts but it was all we could afford and Jim turned me down. In the summer of 2000, Derby allowed him to leave on a free transfer.

In what was effectively the old Third Division, Marc was a really effective player. He could break from midfield; he could play as one of the front two and he scored twice on his home debut against Oxford.

In February 2000, a couple of months before Port Vale were relegated, I had done a deal with Manchester United to bring in David Healy on loan. David had come to Old Trafford as a teenager.

He never quite made it at United but he was a fine footballer who did very well for Preston and Leeds and played nearly 100 times for Northern Ireland.

David had two months with us at Port Vale. He had just turned 20 and didn't drive so I sometimes had to pick him up from Manchester and take him down the M6. I loaned another Manchester United player, Danny Webber, a forward who was to do well at Sheffield United.

When Alex Ferguson reminded me of how he had helped me out, I reminded him that I had loaned him a player first – I had allowed our goalkeeper, Peter Hucker, to go to Old Trafford from Oxford in 1989. He had forgotten, which is something Ferguson rarely did.

There was an awful lot of business done in those years, mostly for free transfers. Michael Cummins, a 22-year-old Irish midfielder, arrived from Middlesbrough and would be remembered for scoring the winner in what at the time of writing is the last Potteries derby with Stoke.

By the summer of 2000, Port Vale had run out of money to finish the Lorne Street Stand and had appointed a Manchester-based barrister, Charles Machin, to the board.

One of Machin's first pronouncements was that by 2010 he wanted to see Port Vale playing Real Madrid on a regular basis. 'My ten-year ambition is to see Vale as one of the top five clubs in Europe,' he said. 'It is my profound belief that the power of God will help get the Vale to the top.'

Machin told me that the players didn't like me, that the tactics were wrong, the training routines were rubbish and that I was being paid too much money. My salary would have been similar to what I had been paid at Brighton. It had been cut when Port Vale were relegated. When I agreed that contract, I was going to a club two divisions higher.

Machin then decided to monitor my training and gave me a long questionnaire that I was supposed to fill out every fortnight and present to the board. It was on how the players performed, what their attitude was, their courage, honesty and even whether they had a sense of humour. The questionnaire had over 60 categories.

Machin told the press that he would be accused of 'making his manager work for his money', adding 'but he does get afternoons off'.

Any director or any fan with even a casual knowledge of football would know that managers do not get afternoons off. You are administering the playing side of the club, you are checking on the youth team and, in the evenings, you often find yourself pounding the motorways bound for a reserve fixture where you might unearth a player. In Port Vale's case a cheap player.

I sent Machin's letters to the League Managers' Association and I told Bill Bell that their response had been outright laughter. To me, it seemed like constructive dismissal. The chief executive of the LMA, John Barnwell, said he had never seen anything like it in his career. John's football career began at Arsenal in 1957.

I stopped Machin one day and said: 'No matter what you do or what you say, I am not walking. The LMA are laughing at you.' Eventually, he was told to take a back seat.

I much preferred working with directors like Alan Jones. His business had been overseeing hygiene in the food industry and he admitted to knowing absolutely nothing about football or footballers. Alan's area of expertise was to oversee the catering at Vale Park, a job he was very good at. He was of far more use to the club than an amateur 'expert' like Charles Machin.

In the middle of all this, Port Vale won the second major piece of silverware in their history. In 1993 they had won the Football League Trophy. In 2001, we won it again. Then it had been sponsored by Auto Windscreens and played at Wembley and now it was the LDV Trophy with the final at the Millennium Stadium in Cardiff.

Port Vale had not enjoyed the cups that season. In the League Cup we had fallen at the first hurdle to Chesterfield and been knocked out of the FA Cup by Canvey Island.

That match would count as the greatest embarrassment of my football career. The game was live on television and Port Vale were 4-2 up with a minute to go. We had missed a penalty into the bargain. Canvey scored a third in the final minute. There were seconds remaining. We kicked off and conceded straight from the kick-off from a long throw.

It was going straight to one of our defenders but the keeper, Mark Goodlad, shouted: 'Leave it.' It was left and one of their players nipped in and equalised. The whole thing was ludicrous.

The replay at Vale Park ought to have finished with us 10-0 up. We explored every avenue when it came to how not to score a goal. The tie went into extra time and Canvey Island scored twice. That concluded two of the worst performances I have been involved with in 50 years of football.

Perhaps that is why we took the Football League Trophy seriously, beating Notts County, Chester and Darlington by an aggregate score of 9-0, which earned us a semi-final against Stoke, which although we were drawn at home, was played at the Britannia Stadium.

The pitch at Vale Park had become so cut up that the fixture kept being postponed until a decision was made to take the game to Stoke. It made the win, which was sealed by Marc Bridge-Wilkinson's penalty, even sweeter.

Bridge-Wilkinson scored another penalty at Sincil Bank against Lincoln in the two-legged Northern Final. Tony Naylor scored another and we played out a goalless draw at Vale Park to take us and 13,000 Vale fans to Cardiff.

This was only the second final the Millennium Stadium had staged while Wembley was being rebuilt – the first was the League Cup Final that saw Liverpool overcome Birmingham on penalties. Over the years, finals at the Millennium Stadium would have a reputation for having a lucky dressing room and a lucky hotel.

The 'lucky' dressing room was the North dressing room, used by Wales for home fixtures. For the first 11 finals the team that had the North dressing room won.

The sequence was broken by Stoke, who won the 2002 League One play-off final from the South dressing room. They were playing Brentford, who a year before had been our opponents in the LDV Final.

The 'lucky' hotel, which was the Vale of Glamorgan, in the countryside outside Cardiff, had an even better run. It was not until 2004, when Middlesbrough won the League Cup against Bolton, that a club staying at the St David's on the Cardiff waterfront took a trophy back. By then the superstition had become so great that the hotels would be chosen by the drawing of lots.

Port Vale won the toss for the North dressing room and we booked the Vale of Glamorgan. Our luck held for about two minutes which was the time it took for Brentford, managed by Ray Lewington, to take the lead.

When we went on to the pitch before the game, the Tannoys were playing the sound of Welsh rugby fans singing and chanting which was a wonderful backdrop. During the half-time interval, my son Matt, shaking with nerves, took part in a fans' penalty shoot-out. I didn't watch, we were still a goal down.

Although we fell behind, Port Vale were the better side throughout and after Tony Naylor had seen his goal disallowed, we won a penalty that Marc Bridge-Wilkinson converted, just as he had against Stoke. Six minutes from the end, Steve Brooker, whom I'd bought from Graham Taylor at Watford for £15,000, scored a screamer to give us the trophy.

The trophy was lifted by Matty Carragher, a player I would take to Macclesfield, a smashing kid and a good footballer who would die tragically young of cancer aged 40.

After we left the stadium, the players asked if they could stay another night, which was the Sunday, at the Vale of Glamorgan. I said no because once we got back, we would be facing games on the Thursday, the Saturday and the Monday. I told them we would go back to the hotel for a drink and ask the chairman to lay on some sandwiches.

The players, with families in tow, went back to the Vale of Glamorgan, where Bill Bell's daughter, Linda, obtained her father's credit card to put behind the bar. She said it was the only time she had been able to get the card off him.

We went to Northampton on the Thursday and won, 2-0. We were mid-table, the play-offs looked pretty distant and I had told the team that, if anyone fancied a rest, I would stand them down for that game.

Everyone wanted to play and, afterwards, David Coates, who had coached me at Luton under David Pleat, phoned to say that was one of the best away performances he had ever seen. We lost, 3-2, to Notts County, beat Bristol Rovers, 3-0, and drew, 1-1, with Oxford in their last game at the Manor Ground. We were not quite good enough to make the play-offs.

By December 2002, all the euphoria from winning the final had long worn off. Port Vale went into administration. The Football League had done a television deal with ITV Digital and the station's collapse dragged a lot of clubs towards the edge.

Port Vale were £2.4m in debt and had lost £500,000 that year. We were mid-table in what would now be League One. There was no danger of us going down but we were unlikely to go up and Robbie Williams decided he did not want to buy the club. Bill Bell called in the receivers.

The impact on me was immediate and it went further than being asked to take a cut in wages. I was told to get rid of Ray Williams, who was my chief scout and someone I'd played alongside when I was at Port Vale in the 1970s. They also wanted me to sack Mark Grew, who had been with the club for 14 years as a goalkeeper and a coach.

I told the administrators that this made no footballing sense but I was informed I would have no choice in the matter. The wage bill had to be drastically and immediately reduced.

It was a horrible time. I said to the administrators, who were based in Birmingham, that in that case they could tell Ray and Mark themselves in the morning. Martin Foyle moved from managing the youth team to being my number two. All we could think of was keeping the club going from week to week and from match to match.

A group of supporters launched a takeover bid, led by Bill Bratt, a former miner who became an insurance broker, and financed by a businessman called Peter Jackson, who lived in Staffordshire. They gained control of the club after a year in administration. Very quickly, it became clear they wanted a new manager.

In February 2004 we beat Sheffield Wednesday, 3-0, at Vale Park to go seventh in the table, one position and one point from a play-off place. After the game, Val came down to my office in tears. I asked her what the problem was.

She said: 'One of the directors has just stopped me at the top of the stairs and told me that on Friday night the directors had a ring round to discuss whether to sack you.'

I was absolutely furious and told Val not to go back upstairs. On the Monday, Sheffield Wednesday sacked their manager, Chris Turner, and I met my chairman, Bill Bratt.

'Did you have a ring round to sack me on Friday?'

'We did because the biggest problem is your wages.'

'You have never discussed my wages with me. If you wanted me to take a pay cut, I would have considered it in return for a longer contract. I can't work with you. I want out. Can you arrange a meeting with Peter Jackson?'

I met Peter Jackson at the Alderley Edge Hotel, told him the situation was intolerable and that I wanted to resign. Jackson agreed to pay me off.

That ended my association with Port Vale, which as a player and a manager had lasted 11 years. It was ironic that both times they should have been in circumstances I had no inkling of.

I had no idea I was about to be sold to Brighton in 1976 and I was oblivious to the fact that firing me had been a burning topic on the board just before we beat Sheffield Wednesday.

Martin Foyle was made caretaker manager and Port Vale missed out on the play-offs on goal difference. The play-offs were won by Brighton.

Silkman

(Games 1,548–1,686)

I WAS not out of work for very long after leaving Port Vale, although when I got a job offer, it was one a lot of people advised me not to take.

The phone call was from Macclesfield Town. They were second from bottom of the Football League and since two clubs would be relegated in May they were three points from safety. There were a few of my friends who told me to steer clear of the Moss Rose. Taking a club out of the Football League would not look good on anyone's CV.

However, when I thought about it, I was a football man, I was out of work and I was well used to firefighting. Who knew when another football job might crop up? David Moss, who had been my assistant at Oxford, Manchester City and Huddersfield, had been in charge at Macclesfield for two years. He told me it was a good club and I should not be afraid of going. I studied the fixture list. There were seven games remaining and the first of those would be at York, who were one place above Macc. There would be other fixtures against teams like Scunthorpe and Rochdale who were in the mix with us and a couple against two of my former clubs, Hull and Oxford, who were pushing for promotion. I backed myself to keep Macclesfield up.

The club was owned by two brothers, Bashar and Amar Alkadhi, who had left Iraq in the 1970s, moved to London and set up a telecommunications company. Bashar's sister-in-law was a big Macclesfield fan and in 2003 they had bought the club. I told them I would take over until the end of the season. Bashar tended to be more involved with the football side of the business and I would talk to him more than to Amar, whose role was more financial. The day-to-day running of the club was done by the chief executive, Colin Garlick, who was to perform the same role at Port Vale.

Matty Carragher, whom I'd managed at Port Vale, was now at Macclesfield but wasn't in the team. Our first game, at York, was the most important of all and I put Matty in as sweeper and played five at the back.

We won, 2-0, at Bootham Crescent with goals from two former York players, Jon Parkin and Graham Potter. Macclesfield were out of the relegation zone on goal difference.

Parkin and Potter were completely different. Graham was one of the quietest men you could hope to meet, Jon was a Yorkshireman who dominated a dressing room. He was an absolute force of nature.

He was loud and very funny. He lived in Barnsley and was often late for training and his kit was often unwashed. His dressing-room banter was usually about what he had just eaten, which tended to be fry-ups, and what he had drunk the night before, which tended to be more than one pint of beer.

You thought to yourself that this was 2004 and things ought to have changed by now but Jon was a very effective centre-forward, who could terrorise defenders.

If you had asked me if one of them would become a manager, I would not have picked Graham. He was and is very intelligent – you would only have to look at his managerial record in Sweden and at Brighton to see that. However, he was so quiet and so reserved at the back of the dressing room that I couldn't see him running a team. It shows not to judge by appearances.

The Moss Rose carried a little reminder of my past. When Maine Road was demolished in 2003, some of the seats had been bought by Macclesfield and put into one of their stands.

My first game there was against Leyton Orient, which we won, 1-0, and then we went to Rochdale and won, 2-1, with both goals scored by Matthew Tipton, a Welshman who led the attack with Parkin. We then drew, 1-1, with Hull, who under Peter Taylor's management would win automatic promotion.

With nine points from four games, Macclesfield were showing promotion form of their own and, although we were only 19th in the table, we were now four places and six points off a relegation place. We secured our future in the Football League with a 2-1 win at home to Oxford courtesy of a couple of own goals. York and Carlisle were relegated.

The way I had planned it, that would be that. I would collect my bonus and look for work somewhere else. I was playing golf one day when Val phoned to say she had just received a large package from Harrods.

'I can absolutely assure you; I have bought you nothing from Harrods,' I replied. I told her to open it up. Inside were six bottles of Krug champagne in individual boxes with a note from Bashar and Amar thanking me for keeping Macclesfield in the Football League.

They called me soon afterwards, asking what my plans were. I told them I was thinking of going on holiday to Las Vegas. I had gone to Vegas on a pre-season tour with Brighton about 25 years before and fancied taking Val there.

Amar told me: 'You book the flights; I'll book the hotel.' They booked us into the Bellagio, on the Strip with enormous fountains in front of the hotel. It was Celine Dion's week off at the Bellagio but they substituted Bryan Adams instead.

It was very hard to say no to them after that. Val and I talked about it in the summer, nobody else had come in for me and I faced the same equation that I had with Brighton six years before. There are only 92 jobs. Financially, their offer was good and it was not far from where I was now living in Cheadle. I got on very well with both brothers and they had secured a decent budget. There was every reason to accept the offer.

I brought in a couple of defenders; Dave Morley, whom I had signed as a youngster for Manchester City, and Danny Swailes, who would eventually be sold to Milton Keynes Dons for £50,000. We won our first three matches and we would be in contention for promotion for the whole season.

In November 2004, I joined the select group of managers who had taken charge of a thousand games. As I write this, there are 31 of us. They are listed on the League Managers' Association website in alphabetical order from Sam Allardyce to Danny Wilson. The names include Sir Alex Ferguson, Arsène Wenger, Carlo Ancelotti, Sir Matt Busby and Sir Bobby Robson – plus my old neighbour, Jim Smith.

Twenty years after my first match as a manager, a goalless draw between Lincoln and Hull, my thousandth game was in the Football League Trophy, against Mansfield at the Moss Rose. Perhaps you could have asked for a grander game but I couldn't have asked for a better result. We won, 4-0, with Parkin and Tipton scoring three of the four.

Between 15 January, when we beat Kidderminster, 2-0, and 19 March, when we beat Leyton Orient 3-1, Macclesfield won nine games out of 11. We were third in the League Two table, three points off the top club, Yeovil, with a game in hand.

Our next match was on a Friday night against Swansea at the Vetch Field which was in its last season before the move to the Liberty Stadium. Even when they were in the old Fourth Division, I had always had great respect for Swansea's fans.

They were loud and passionate and right opposite the dressing rooms, there was a big stand full of home supporters. I pointed to it and said to the players: 'Don't do anything stupid in front of there. I don't want those fans riled and putting pressure on the ref.'

Before half-time, Jon Parkin, who was getting irritated by the treatment he was receiving from Swansea's centre-half, Izzy Iriekpen, smashed the ball into the crowd – he was supposed to be aiming at our left-back to take a throw in. The ball hit a young lad full in the face and he needed treatment by the St John Ambulance.

Then, in the second half, right in front of the stand, where I had told everyone to keep calm, Parkin slid in to clatter Iriekpen. The crowd went wild and Jon was shown a straight red card. The 2-0 defeat was bad but what was worse was that we lost our best striker for three matches.

We drew all three but managed only two goals and fell out of the automatic promotion places. Macclesfield had also lost a momentum which we never quite got back. On Parkin's return we lost, 2-0, at Lincoln and 2-1 to a last-minute goal at home to Southend.

Macclesfield missed out on automatic promotion by five points and I still feel that had Jon Parkin not got himself sent off at Swansea we would have been promoted. At that level Jon was such a good player that when on song he could be the difference between one point and three and sometimes no points and three.

We drew Lincoln in the play-off semi-finals. Lincoln were managed by Keith Alexander, who was appointed to manage Macclesfield in 2008 and was just about to take charge of his 100th game for the club when he died suddenly at the age of 53.

Under Keith, Lincoln were a very powerful side who excelled at set pieces and Gareth McAuley headed in a free-kick early on, while Matthew Tipton hit the bar for Macc. We were 1-0 down going into the second leg but McAuley scored another header and, although we drew the game, that was as far as our season went.

In the summer of 2005, I signed Martin Bullock, who had played for Barnsley in the Premier League and had won two Football League trophies at Blackpool under Steve McMahon. I was confident that this time Macclesfield could win promotion automatically.

We began with a pre-season friendly against Manchester City. It was a good money-spinner for the club but it cost us our biggest asset. Jon Parkin went up for a header with Richard Dunne, landed awkwardly, and suffered a knee ligament injury. It would be late October before Parkin could play again. Matthew Tipton, who had formed such a fine partnership with Parkin, had left for Mansfield, who could pay him more than we could afford. Our forward line was now severely depleted.

By the time Parkin made his return in a 2-1 win over Bristol Rovers, we were bottom of the Football League. One of the few bright spots had been beating Nottingham Forest, 3-2, in the League Cup but there had been very few others. Now came an upswing.

In the space of two-and-a-half weeks in December we put four past Cambridge in the Football League Trophy and won, 5-4, at Wycombe. On Boxing Day, we thrashed Stockport, 6-0, while missing a penalty. Chris Turner was managing Stockport and he was sacked immediately afterwards, just as he had been when Port Vale had beaten Sheffield Wednesday in my final game for the club. I had done something similar to Ossie Ardiles.

It was the biggest win in Macclesfield's history and at the start of the year we had beaten Notts County, 5-0, at Meadow Lane, which meant I had managed the club to their biggest home and away victories. The win over Notts County was one of the best performances I have seen in my thousand-plus games as a football manager. I didn't say anything to the team when they came back into the dressing room. I just applauded.

In January 2006, Jon scored his final goal for Macclesfield in a 3-1 defeat at Boston. It was then that we received a bid from Hull, who were in the Championship. They were prepared to pay £250,000 and more than double Jon's wages, which at Macclesfield were £1,300 a week. Parkin threatened to go on strike unless we did the deal.

Frankly, there was no need to threaten us. It was one of those transfer bids – like Sheffield Wednesday's for Andy

Booth when I was at Huddersfield – that you knew your club could not turn down.

This was especially true of Macclesfield in 2006. A few years before, under different ownership, they had spent £1.5m on a new stand. The club had cut £245,000 from the bill by asking the builders, Alfred McAlpine, to sponsor the stand for ten years. The FA ruled this was illegal and now Macclesfield had to pay the money back plus a fine.

In my first season I had been pretty generously funded by the Alkadhis. The budget was approaching £1.2m but after we failed to go through the play-offs and once the FA demanded we pay nearly £300,000, it began steadily reducing and our performances reduced with them.

As it was, the knee Jon had injured against Manchester City meant he failed his medical at Hull. Peter Taylor changed his offer from a 30-month contract to an 18-month one. We still got our money and it didn't prevent Jon scoring on his debut against Crystal Palace.

The finances meant you would often have to take a chance with a footballer. Early on in my time at Macc, we signed Wayne Rooney's cousin, Tommy, which did not really work and he went back to playing non-league football with Vauxhall Motors. Through their contacts in Iraq, the Alkadhis brought over Jassim Swadi, who had been playing in Baghdad and was an Iraq international midfielder.

He never settled and found Ramadan especially tough. As a Muslim during Ramadan you cannot eat or drink during daylight and in northern England in August there can be a lot of daylight. The lads who roomed with him on away trips told me he preferred to sleep on the floor and he could not adapt to the English game. He was homesick – as you or I would be had we just been uprooted to the Middle East – and eventually we allowed him to go back to Baghdad.

Macclesfield may have been on the slide in the league but in the FA Trophy we put together a series of results that took us one game away from the final at the Millennium Stadium.

We had beaten Chesterfield, Rotherham, Cambridge and Hereford to reach the Northern final against Carlisle. Just to emphasise how small a world football can be, Paul Simpson, whom I'd managed at Oxford, was now in charge of Carlisle and his assistant was Dennis Booth, who had been my number two at Hull and Huddersfield.

At Brunton Park, we took the lead when Andy Smart scored his only goal for Macc. It was some goal – a shot that flew into the net from 22 yards. We were holding on for a 1-1 draw when in the 93rd minute, the referee, Nigel Miller, awarded Carlisle a corner when everyone in the ground knew it was a goal kick. On the bench, you could almost sense what was coming. The corner comes in, Peter Murphy heads it home from six yards and we have lost, 2-1. I went berserk at the final whistle which followed a few seconds after the header struck the net.

There was still the second leg to play at the Moss Rose and we gave it a very good go. After 28 minutes we were 2-0 up but Carlisle scored before half-time and at 2-1 it went into extra time and finished 3-2 to Macclesfield. We went out on the away-goals rule.

Paul and Dennis took Carlisle to the final in Cardiff, where they lost, 2-1, to Swansea. The season fizzled out. Macclesfield finished 17th in League Two while my old club, Oxford, with Jim Smith, at the helm, fell out of the Football League.

There was always a need to bring in money to Macclesfield and in the summer I phoned Sir Alex Ferguson to ask if he would be prepared to bring a Manchester United side to the Moss Rose for a pre-season friendly.

At the time, I got on very well with Alex. I used to play golf with him and we would see him and Cathy socially. He agreed immediately. Macclesfield had never played Manchester United before and it was going to be a big occasion in the town. We needed to advertise the match and had to have some idea of who would be playing for Manchester United. So, it was with a little bit of trepidation that I phoned Alex again to ask who would play.

He said: 'Rooney, Ferdinand, van der Sar.' I said: 'Are you serious?'

'Yeah, they're coming back from the World Cup, they're going to need games.'

He was as good as his word. There were about 5,500 at the Moss Rose which was the biggest crowd Macc had seen for years. I may have paid for a year of my salary with a couple of phone calls. I told Bashar to give Fergie the best bottle of red wine he could find. Wayne Rooney scored the first goal and Fraizer Campbell, whom I was to work with at Hull, got the second in a 2-1 win.

There were not many memorable afternoons to follow. We lost our opening league game, 4-0, at Darlington and things didn't get much better. By the time Macclesfield had lost at Hereford on 30 September we had four points from 12 games and were bottom of the Football League, seven points adrift of the next lowest club, Boston United. I was sacked.

This was the second season which I'd prepared for by having to cut costs, get rid of players who were on good money (for the division) and bring in footballers on lower wages. There is only so far you can travel down that road and by September 2006 I was in a dead-end street. It was time to go.

The Alkadhis brothers gave Paul Ince his first chance in football management. Macclesfield did not win a game until 5 December but, against all the odds, they managed to save themselves right at the death.

Five years later, Macclesfield got in touch again and asked if I would come back to the Moss Rose, repeat what I had done first time around and keep them in the Football League.

I should immediately have said no but I didn't. There have not been too many regrets in my football career but going back to Macc was one of them. On the surface, they looked in better shape than the club I had taken over in 2004 – then they had been second from bottom and now they were two places better off.

The looks were deceptive. Macclesfield had won a single league game in five months and were in complete freefall. You didn't have to spend much time with the players to realise they were not good enough to stop the slide. In 2004, there had been a nucleus around which you could rebuild but in 2012 it simply wasn't there.

This time I had nine matches to save them and all we managed were two draws. At home to Port Vale, we had a penalty to take the lead and I watched it being blazed over the bar and almost out of the ground. Port Vale won the game with a goal eight minutes from time. We took the lead against Crewe and Nick Powell, who would earn a transfer to Old Trafford from Gresty Road, scored twice. We pulled it back to 2-2 but it was never enough. You knew what was coming.

A 2-0 defeat against Burton at the Moss Rose saw us relegated. There was one more game to go, at Southend, but there was no point in my staying.

After I'd left Macclesfield for the first time in 2006, I wondered just where my career might go or even if it was over. I was 57, I still thought of myself as someone with something to offer but in football careers can end without you knowing it. Suddenly, you think to yourself that you might not be part of the game anymore.

I knew Phil Brown, though not as a friend. I had first met him at Old Trafford watching a reserve game. He was working as Sam Allardyce's assistant and they had taken Bolton from the Championship to the Premier League, into Europe and to a League Cup Final.

Phil is someone whose conversation consists of asking you a thousand questions. He has an eagerness to learn from whoever he is speaking to. He said to me: 'I want to be a manager in my own right, what do you think?'

I told him to take a look at where he was. In the heart of the Premier League, working alongside Sam in a brand-new stadium and with a job that seemed totally secure. 'No,' he said. 'I want to be a manager. I want to prove to myself I can do it.'

'If that's really what you want to do, then do it. Otherwise, you will regret it for the rest of your life.'

The next time I saw him, I was out of work and we met at a sportsmen's lunch in Manchester. He asked me what I was doing – he would have known I hadn't worked since leaving Macclesfield.

Since we had last spoken, Phil had left Bolton and tried his hand at management with Derby. That had been something of a disaster but he had taken over at Hull and had pulled them out of the relegation zone in the Championship.

He said: 'If I keep Hull up, I've been promised the job and I want an experienced number two. Would you consider working as my assistant?' I said I couldn't tell him there and then. The only time I'd been a number two was with Mark Lawrenson at Oxford in 1988. That had been nearly 20 years earlier.

Phil had taken over at the KC Stadium in December 2006 with Hull second bottom and five points from safety. He kept them up and in May he was offered the job permanently. It was then that I got a call to ask if I would meet him and talk football.

We met at the Marriott at Worsley, which is a hotel a lot of football people use because it is close to Manchester and just off the motorway. We had a sandwich and a coffee and talked about how we saw the game. He also wanted Val and I to have a meal with him and his wife, Karen, to see how we would get on, which showed an interesting side to Phil's outlook.

Phil told me that he would be interviewing six people around my age – Denis Smith and Colin Todd were two names he mentioned. Long before I had met Phil Brown, I had thought this was good business.

If you are a young manager, instead of appointing someone your own age, why not bring in someone who has seen and done things you haven't or who can give you a different perspective? Although it did not end well, Steve McClaren's decision to appoint Terry Venables as his assistant manager with England was a good one.

My daughter, Lucy, was at John Moores University in Liverpool and Val and I took her out to dinner in Bramhall. Whenever I didn't have a club the twins would invariably ask if there were any offers or whether I was close to anything. They knew I was a different person to be around when I had a job.

'There might be a chance of me going back to where you were born, in Hull,' I told her. 'I've had a talk with Phil Brown but, to tell the truth, he has never got back to me so I don't know.'

The moment I had said those words, my phone rang. It was Phil Brown, offering me the job. The call was the start of one of my longest relationships in football.

Tiger Two

(Games 1,687–1,816)

I WAS on the coach going to Wembley for the play-off final with the black-and-gold colours of Hull City everywhere. Phil Brown was in the seat next to me.

Hull had never been in the top flight before and the expectation was enormous. Then, in 2008, the game was said to be worth £60m to the winners. Now, that sum has more than doubled.

'Nobby, what do you think?' the manager said. 'This could be a life-changing game of football.'

I turned to him and said: 'Phil, there is no way we will lose this game.'

There were reasons for my confidence. We had finished the season well, we were the form team, the one everyone dreads meeting in the play-offs.

It had been an up-and-down, rollercoaster of a season. With a quarter of the games gone, we were 13th, 14 points behind the leaders, Watford.

At the halfway mark, Hull had climbed slightly to 11th. We were now 12 points behind Watford but as the division tightened at the top, we were five points from a play-off place.

By 2 March, the season was three-quarters done. We had just lost 1-0 at Bristol City, the new league leaders. There were 14 points between us and Bristol City but only two between ourselves and Ipswich, who were in the final play-off position and we had a game in hand.

Hull won eight of their next 11 games. We played in a 4-4-2 formation, we were solid and aggressive. People like Jay-Jay Okocha and Henrik Pedersen could not get in the team.

We put five past Southampton, we beat Leicester 2-0 and Watford 3-0. After Fraizer Campbell and Ian Ashbee had given us a 2-1 win over Crystal Palace, we were third with one game left.

West Bromwich Albion's goal difference was so great, they were certain to go up but we could still catch Stoke. It would need Hull to win at Ipswich and Stoke to lose at home to Leicester. Stoke drew. Hull lost at Portman Road. It was the play-offs and the semi-final would see us play Watford.

Before the game at Vicarage Road, we stayed at the Grove, a beautiful hotel which England use before games at Wembley, and Arsène Wenger had given us permission to use the Arsenal training ground at London Colney. The pitches, needless to say, were immaculate.

We fancied ourselves to beat Watford, who had not finished the season well, and we did, though it should have been by a greater margin than 2-0. Ian Ashbee hit the post and Fraizer should have scored after being clean through. In the dressing room afterwards, the feeling was that the tie should already have been put to bed.

The KC Stadium was packed for the second leg. They were expectant and noisy. Very soon, they became quiet and anxious. Watford under Aidy Boothroyd tended to play only one way. They played 4-4-2 and liked a long ball.

Up in the stands, the first thing I noticed was that Boothroyd had changed the system for the second leg. They were now in a diamond and Watford scored early on and should probably have had more than one goal. They were murdering us and we didn't seem to know how to cope.

Fortunately, Nicky Barmby, who had the experience you often desperately need in situations like these, popped up with a goal before half-time. It calmed everyone down. We scored three times in the last 20 minutes to win 6-1 on aggregate. Hull would be playing Bristol City, who had beaten Crystal Palace 4-2.

For the final, we wanted to replicate what we had done for the Watford game. However, when we phoned the Grove, the hotel told us that England would be staying there, preparing to play the United States in a friendly. They said Fabio Capello would not allow any other team to use the Grove.

I rang someone at the FA who confirmed that we would not be allowed to stay at the hotel. I said: 'I wonder if Mr Capello appreciates what an important game this is for Hull City. We have never been promoted this far and we want to replicate everything we did for the semi-final.' She said she would put it to him.

She came back to me and said: 'Mr Capello does appreciate this is a very important game for Hull so you can stay at the Grove, provided you keep to one part of the hotel.'

However, we couldn't train at Arsenal's ground because England had taken over London Colney. The Grove did, however, have a small football pitch at the back of the hotel so we trained on that. When we were having our pre-match meal before going to Wembley, Capello came in and wished us all good luck which I thought was a lovely gesture.

The people going on to that bus to Wembley were men you had confidence in. Ian Ashbee, a fantastic leader whom I had a great relationship with, would captain Hull in every division. Boaz Myhill kept goal for Hull in every division. Andy Dawson had been signed by Peter Taylor when Hull were in the bottom division and he played left-back in the Premier League. His brother, Michael, played centre-half for Tottenham and for Hull under Steve Bruce.

In our years at the KC Stadium we would look at Andy and wonder if the step-up would be too much for him but he proved us wrong every time. Perhaps the best two results in our time in the Premier League came when we played back-to-back away games against Arsenal and then Tottenham.

We won both. In the first, Andy was up against Theo Walcott and in the second Tottenham had Aaron Lennon on the wing. Dawson was exceptional in both games.

Andy was from Northallerton in north Yorkshire and had a great friendship with Nicky Barmby, who like Dean Windass had come back to Humberside where their football careers had begun. They were experienced and they were motivated and they were exactly the kind of attributes Hull City required.

Nicky was 33 when the season started and he had played more than 300 Premier League games for Tottenham, Middlesbrough, Everton, Liverpool and Leeds. We would play him on the left wing at Hull but he could and would go anywhere, sometimes playing off the front two. He had an exceptional football brain and was ultra-professional. He had played at Wembley which is something I had never done as a player or a manager.

Dean was 38. At Bradford, he had been part of Paul Jewell's side that won promotion to the Premier League and had beaten Liverpool on the final day of the season to stay up.

More than 20 years before, I had released him from Hull, his hometown club, the one he had always dreamed of playing for. When I let him go, I had ended my talk by telling him: 'I know you will prove me wrong.'

Dean mirrored what I had done when I was let go by Walsall. Like me, he had been released because he was considered too small and not had enough pace. He had the skill but not the mobility. He went to play non-league football for North Ferriby, worked on a building site and dragged himself back up. When I met him again, Dean said it did him good. It enabled him to regain his focus.

Whenever I took training, I would ask some of the forwards to stay behind to practise their finishing and just before we went to the Grove to prepare for the final Deano came over and asked if I could do some finishing work with him.

I said: 'No way am I doing that. I am terrified you're going to pull your thigh muscle. No chance.'

In the 38th minute of the final, I was very glad I'd been cautious. Fraizer Campbell chipped a ball from just outside the Bristol City six-yard box and Deano volleyed it into the net from the edge of the area. It ensured he will be a hero in Hull for the rest of his life.

One thing that struck me as I watched the game was that our fans were in the sunshine all afternoon while those who had come from Bristol were in shade.

It was a tense game towards the end and there were some great defensive blocks by Michael Turner and Sam Ricketts but we deserved the win.

We went back to the Grove where they set up a beach bar in the grounds and some of the team – Deano included – drank through the night.

When we went through the city on an open-topped bus the next day, Dean was still drunk from all the celebrations and when he stepped on to a ledge on the Town Hall to take the applause, some of us were terrified he would fall.

The celebrations across Humberside were astonishing. Hull had been in the bottom division five years before and their rise to the top flight was the joint-quickest in the history of the Football League. Northampton between 1960 and 1965 and Fulham (1996–2001) also went from the bottom to the top in five years.

It was not just the players who were responsible for the rise. Hull had a very good backroom staff who had been there long before Phil and I came to the KC Stadium.

Phil Hough was the club secretary. Barry Lowe was the kit man and Barry's wife, who had been in charge of the laundry when I was managing Hull in the 1980s, was still there. Steve Parkin, who had managed Rochdale in his own right and who I still speak to most weeks, was first-team coach. Bronwen and Sally were secretaries to Phil Hough and Phil Brown.

Billy Russell ran the youth team alongside Neil Mann. Simon Maltby was a superb physio. Sean Rush, who had supported Hull all his life, was the fitness coach. Mark Prudhoe was our goalkeeping coach. In my career I have never seen any man work so hard. He coached every age group at Hull from under-11s upwards. That summed up the work ethic we had. It was a wonderful team and Hull's rise from the bottom to the top was because of people like them.

When I was asked to go to Humberside, the chairman was Adam Pearson, who had left his job as commercial director at Leeds United to take over at Hull, who were then in administration. Pearson oversaw the move from Boothferry

Park to the KC Stadium and in the summer of 2007, just after I had signed a contract with the club, he sold out to Paul Duffen and Russell Bartlett. Paul became Hull's new chairman.

Phil and I were called to a meeting at the Forest Pines hotel, just over the Humber Bridge in Lincolnshire. Paul and Russell told us they had a three-year plan for the club, which then had just avoided relegation to League One.

In the first year they would invest – not big money but enough to keep us in the division. With that money we bought Richard Garcia and Wayne Brown from Colchester, Dean Windass, Nicky Barmby and Bryan Hughes.

When I was at Huddersfield, Bryan had impressed when we played Wrexham and I tried to take him to the McAlpine. I was prepared to go as high as £500,000 but Trevor Francis offered £1m and he went to Birmingham. Ten years later, Bryan came on a free transfer from Charlton.

The second year would see them fund a more significant rebuild and our target would be a top-half finish in the Championship. They expected us to have a serious push for promotion in year three. We carried out the three-year plan in a single season.

The three-year plan began in the Italian Alps in Bormio where, when Phil was assistant to Sam Allardyce, Bolton had often done their pre-season training.

What happened in that week in the Alps is, I am convinced, the key to Hull's transformation from relegation candidates to a Premier League team in a single season. It forged a bond not just among the players but with the staff. When we gathered to fly to Italy from East Midlands Airport, I barely knew anyone at the club.

At six in the morning, the squad got up to prepare for a bike ride through the mountains. I was excused because of my age and Simon Maltby our physio was excused because he did not want to do it.

Then, they would have breakfast and train in the morning, have lunch, followed by a training session in the evening. Bormio is an astonishingly beautiful place. In the mornings you would see a gentle mist on the mountains, then it would clear to let you see the snowline in the sunshine.

Paul Duffen flew to Bormio to meet the players and joined in the tennis and the golf competitions. We let the players out for one night.

It was only in the last half of the season that Hull really clicked. Early on, there was seldom a pattern to our results. We began with a 3-2 home defeat to Plymouth and won just one of our first five games.

A turning point came in December when we lost 3-0 at Preston and followed that up with a 4-0 defeat at Southampton. Hull were almost as close to a relegation place as we were to a play-off place.

I told Phil: 'If we keep playing like that, we are going to get the sack.' We decided we could not afford to keep playing Jay-Jay Okocha in every game. Okocha had a great impact on the training ground and was brilliant in eight v eight games but on a big pitch, where he had to run, he was becoming less effective because he was 34 years old.

Henrik Pedersen, who was another player Phil had managed at Bolton, was also moved to the sidelines. Instead of a diamond or a 4-3-3, we would go 4-4-2, which made us much harder to beat, although there were still a few hiccups.

One of them came in the FA Cup, where we were beaten, 3-2, at Plymouth. We had flown down to Devon on the Friday and the journey was seriously scary. The plane was pitched and tossed by the wind and for most of the journey our captain, Ian Ashbee, had his head in his hands, crouched in the brace position in his seat.

Less than a month later, in early February, we were due to go to Plymouth again for a league fixture. Ian Ashbee went to see the manager and told Phil Brown that the players did not want to fly.

Phil was incredulous: 'You would rather have a seven-hour journey on a coach from Hull to Plymouth rather than spend 45 minutes on a plane?'

Ian said: 'Yes. The players don't want it.' We embarked on a 14-hour round trip and won, 1-0, with a goal from Dean Windass.

The first meeting I had to talk about recruitment was with Phil Brown and the chief scout, Bob Shaw, at Tankersley Manor near Sheffield. One of the first names that was on my lips and Bob's was Fraizer Campbell.

I first came across him at a Manchester United reserve game. Gerard Pique, who had just been signed from Barcelona's youth team, was also playing.

I met Alex Ferguson at the game and he asked me to sit with him. Campbell was playing right wing and I had never seen him before. He was quick, strong, dynamic and Alex turned to me and said: 'He's going to be a good player.' From Alex Ferguson, that kind of understated comment was high praise. Bob had also seen Campbell play and said much the same thing.

In July, Manchester United played Port Vale in a pre-season friendly and Bob went to see Fraizer perform with Phil Brown. He scored in a game that Port Vale won, 3-2. It was enough to convince us to make a phone call. Phil said: 'You know Fergie better than me, why don't you give him a call.'

When I phoned, Alex said there was no chance of a deal. He rated Campbell and he wanted him to play in Manchester United's League Cup games and perhaps those Champions League group matches when United were already through.

However, in September, the month Campbell turned 20, Manchester United were beaten at home by Coventry in their first fixture in the League Cup and Phil said to me: 'Fraizer's hardly going to be playing now, why don't you give Fergie another call?'

When I phoned again the answer was yes. Phil and the chairman, Paul Duffen, met Ferguson at Aintree Racecourse

– where we had taken the players and staff for a day out – to discuss the deal. He scored twice on his home debut against Barnsley and 15 times in his first season at Hull. For most of the promotion season, Fraizer would be leading the attack with Dean Windass.

Like my dad, Bob Shaw had been a miner and he and his wife, Bet, were people I got on very well with. There were some scouting trips that took us further afield than watching Manchester United reserve games.

One I shall always remember was to Cairo not because of who we signed – I cannot even recall who we were supposed to be watching – but the absolute absurdity of it all.

The player's agent had picked us up in what was the oldest car I have ever sat in. He drove us to a 50,000-seater stadium, which was almost completely empty to watch a very mundane game of football.

The player we were interested in was patently not good enough for Hull City. As politely as we could, Bob and I explained to the agent that we didn't need to talk to the player and the agent offered to drive us back to the hotel.

The traffic in Cairo is bad enough at the best of times but the agent was weaving this old jalopy through the streets at what seemed like 100mph. When we were dropped off, I turned to Bob and said: 'If you ever suggest going to Egypt again, I am retiring on the spot.'

Once Hull were in the Premier League, the targets became bigger. When he was working with Sam Allardyce,

Phil became adept at bringing in foreign players who would not have dreamed of playing for Bolton Wanderers.

Bob Shaw had very good contacts in France and one of our targets was Adil Rami, who was then 22, playing for Lille at centre-half. He would go on to play for Valencia and AC Milan and would later become Pamela Anderson's other half. After we recommended him, Bob took Phil to watch him play but Phil wasn't convinced and the moment came and went.

Edinson Cavani was another who nearly came to Hull. In the summer of 2009, after we had stayed up in the Premier League, Bob and I went to Sicily to watch him play for Palermo. We tabled a bid of £2.5 million which met Palermo's valuation but then a lot of much bigger clubs became involved and the transfer became very messy. Cavani eventually decided to stay in Sicily and joined Napoli the following season. In 2013, he was transferred to Paris St Germain for £55 million.

We came closer to landing Alvaro Negredo. The striker wasn't getting games at Real Madrid after joining them from Almeria so Bob Shaw and I became involved again. Paul Duffen and I met Negredo's agent – who also represented Jozy Altidore whom we had taken on loan from Villarreal.

The deal for Negredo was that we would take him from Real Madrid for £12m and Real would buy him back for £13m. However, Negredo decided to sign for Seville and joined Manchester City in 2013. We might not have got Rami, Cavani or Negredo but it does demonstrate what a good scout Bob was and that Hull and their board did not lack ambition.

Phil was always interested in new ideas. We travelled to Bahrain to meet their FA to discuss a joint venture and we signed up to play in the Premier League's Asia Trophy in Beijing alongside Tottenham and West Ham. The clubs would be paid £500,000 between them to take part.

Phil was very much into statistics and on the Friday he would take the team training to practise one or two specific routines. On the day before a game he wanted the players to hear only one voice, his own.

There were plenty of team-bonding trips. In May 2009, we had not won in nine Premier League games and we were at Bolton for the penultimate match of the season. Phil arranged an outward-bound course in the Lake District. It was cold, damp and wet and Steve Parkin managed to turn me, Simon Maltby and himself over in a canoe. Significantly, perhaps, we drew the game at the Reebok Stadium and that point was the difference in our survival.

He would talk to the captain, Ian Ashbee, and between them they would give the players plenty of freedom. Whether it was archery or mountain biking, Sam Ricketts seemed to be the one who always excelled on those days out.

When I started working with him, Phil said to me: 'I don't want a yes man. I want you to say what you think.' He wanted to bounce ideas off me and Steve Parkin, who had also been a manager. Phil said that one of the reasons he failed at Derby was because he didn't have someone with whom he could do that.

I had no intention of being Phil Brown's yes man. I was living in Cheshire and Hull had provided Phil with a house in Ferriby so I moved in with him and we would go out to the pub or to a snooker place that I remembered from when I was living there in the 1980s.

We would have fall-outs because I would tell him what I thought. Occasionally, the arguments would get so bad that I would get in my car and drive home. We were like an old married couple.

In one way, going up to the Premier League via the play-offs is the best way to win promotion because it is so memorable. However, because you go up later than anyone else, Hull were guaranteed a frantic summer.

Because of my links to Manchester City and the fact I lived in Cheshire, I would go there quite regularly. In the summer of 2008, City replaced Sven Göran Eriksson with Mark Hughes as their manager and he got rid of some of Sven's players, including the Brazilian forward, Geovanni.

He was 28 and had played for Barcelona and Benfica and had scored the winner for City in the Manchester derby but when he was released Geovanni had not scored a goal in five months. He was available on a free transfer.

I rang Les Chapman, who was now Manchester City's kit man but who had been a coach when I was at Maine Road and had performed the same role when I was at Huddersfield. He knew his football.

Les said he had no idea why Manchester City had let him go. His ability was unquestionable. We set up a meeting with his agent and Paul Duffen and Phil Brown sealed the deal.

In pre-season we went to Belgium to play Ostend and Geovanni scored a wonder-goal, something typically Brazilian. He lived in Alderley Edge, he had a driver and I would sometimes travel across to Yorkshire with him while he slept in the back.

Hull's first game in the top flight was at home to Fulham. We fell behind early on but Geovanni then took control of the ball, ran at the Fulham goal, and shot past Mark Schwarzer from 20 yards. In the second half, Caleb Folan had a tap-in to give us a win in our first match.

He liked the big games. In late September, we went to Arsenal, who were then top of the Premier League. Once again, we fell behind and then Geovanni struck a goal that was probably better than the one he scored against Fulham. It was hit from 20 yards from the left-hand edge of the area and flew past Manuel Almunia. Daniel Cousin headed our winner from a corner.

The following Sunday we went to Tottenham and Geovanni scored the winner after nine minutes with a free kick from nearly 30 yards. After seven games, Hull were third in the Premier League, three points ahead of the champions, Manchester United. That start was crucial to our survival. After nine games we had 20 points. We finished with 35.

One of the reasons was that Geovanni did not enjoy an English winter, which on Humberside could be bitter. Geovanni would come to the training pitches in a hat, gloves and wrapped in an overcoat.

In November, he scored the equaliser at home to Manchester City which would have given him a lot of pleasure but he did not score again for another four months. That goal was vital because it was in a 1-1 draw with Newcastle, who were to become our rivals in the battle to survive in the Premier League.

On Boxing Day came a moment for which Phil Brown will be forever remembered. It was the day he delivered his half-time team-talk to the players on the pitch at the Etihad Stadium.

It looked bizarre but the background to it was that Phil had given the players Christmas Day off. That was a rare thing to do. I had done it at Brighton simply because so few of our players actually lived in the town and they were being paid peanuts. Usually, I would ask my squad to train on Christmas Day if we were playing the next afternoon.

On matchdays, I would be miked up with an earpiece so I could sit in the stands and give Phil advice, if it was needed, about any changes to the opposition's formation or suggestions about how we might alter our tactics.

We were getting absolutely smashed by Manchester City. We were four down after 36 minutes, Robinho had scored twice. Phil said to me: 'I am going to keep them on the pitch during the interval.'

I said: 'What?'

'They have let me down.'

I told him that he should do what he thought was best. He sat them not far from where the Hull City fans were and all he said to them was: 'You have let me down, you have let yourselves down,' and then pointing to our fans, he said: 'You have let them down. Do something about it in the second half.'

Phil got an awful lot of stick for that and from an awful lot of angles. However, the facts were that we 'drew the second half'. The final score was 5-1. If Brian Clough had done it, people might have called it a stroke of genius. If Alan Mullery had told me he was going to conduct his half-time talk on the pitch while I was at Brighton, I would have stayed on the pitch and listened to him.

Several years later, when we were at Southend, we had just won at Milton Keynes Dons. The coach would take the players back to Essex and Phil and I would take the train from Milton Keynes to Manchester because we both lived in the North West.

The coach dropped us by the station and we looked for somewhere to have a beer. Someone at the station suggested we go to an Indian restaurant for one.

The owner recognised Phil and he came over for a chat and the guy said: 'Would you do your team-talk at Manchester City for my staff?' In the centre of the restaurant, where there were people dining, the owner gathered all his staff and told them to sit in the middle of the floor.

Phil stood in the middle and pointed at one of the waiters and said: 'You need a haircut. It's a disgrace your coming to work like that.' To another, he said: 'Why are you unshaven?' The diners in the restaurant must have thought everyone had gone mad.

Afterwards, the owner prepared a little banquet of Indian food for us to take on the train back to Manchester.

In our first season in the Premier League, we had a good run in the FA Cup, beating Newcastle, Millwall and Sheffield United to reach the quarter-finals, where we drew Arsenal away.

Because we had beaten them at the Emirates in the league, there was a lot of tension surrounding the fixture. Hull had not been to an FA Cup semi-final since 1930 when they had been beaten by Arsenal after a replay.

Now, at the Emirates Stadium, Nicky Barmby had given us the lead and we stayed in front until almost a quarter of an hour from the end when Robin van Persie hit an equaliser. We were six minutes from a replay when William Gallas scored from a blatantly offside position.

Right at the end, Anthony Gardner, who had been pushed up from centre-half to centre-forward in an attempt to get an equaliser, was smashed in the back. Cesc Fabregas had not been involved in the game but was sitting on the bench in jeans, a hoodie and a leather jacket.

He walked over near to where Anthony Gardner was receiving treatment. He had a row with Sean Rush and, as we were going into the tunnel, I was convinced he spat at me. The game had been on television and none of the 28 cameras at the game picked it up.

I was angry but I thought it wouldn't go any further until I was in the car driving away from the Emirates Stadium – the team bus was headed back to Yorkshire and we were returning to the North West.

Suddenly the incident came on the radio and I said to Phil: 'Did you mention it in the press conference?'

He said: 'Yes I did. I am not having people spitting at you. Do you want to take this any further?'

I told him I did and eventually, after a hearing, Fabregas was cleared of improper conduct as the FA could not be certain he was spitting directly at me. However, what nobody seemed to consider was the fact that Fabregas should not have been on the bench and certainly should not have been on the pitch.

Just before the quarter-final, Hull had gone to Craven Cottage and beaten Fulham, 1-0. With ten games to go, we were 12th, comfortably mid-table. We did not win another match.

The only three points we got in those last two months came from Geovanni's goal against Newcastle, a goalless draw at home to Portsmouth and that draw against Bolton after Phil had taken everyone off to the Lake District.

On the morning of the last day of the season, West Brom were already relegated and unless Middlesbrough thrashed West Ham at Upton Park and everyone around them lost, they would be joining them in the Championship. Realistically, they too were down.

There were three of us fighting to avoid the last relegation place. Newcastle, who were managed by Alan Shearer with Iain Dowie assisting him, had 34 points. They were at Aston Villa.

Hull had 35 and above us were Sunderland, who were recovering from Roy Keane's decision to walk out on the club, with 36. We were both at home but Sunderland would be playing Chelsea and we would be facing the champions, Manchester United.

Chelsea won, 3-2. There had been some talk that Manchester United, who were preparing for a Champions League Final against Barcelona, might go easy on us but there was no chance of that. They won, 1-0, thanks to a fabulous strike from Darron Gibson.

Because so many fans had gone to Villa Park from Tyneside, Newcastle's kick-off had been delayed. They were losing, 1-0, thanks to an own goal from Damien Duff but, if they equalised, we would be relegated on goal difference.

It was like being back at Tranmere with Oxford; we were standing by the pitch waiting for a result. Then it came through that Newcastle had lost and Phil grabbed a microphone and began singing the chorus of the Beach Boys' hit, 'Sloop John B' in front of the crowd. He liked to perform; he sang at the Player of the Year dinner.

Our second season in the Premier League had nothing like this kind of happy ending. Hull started the new season like they finished the old one. We lost 2-1 at Stamford Bridge to a last-minute goal from Didier Drogba and we were then hammered 5-1 at home by Tottenham. Liverpool beat us 6-1 at Anfield and we went down 4-1 at Sunderland.

In October, Paul Duffen had left the club after the old owner, Adam Pearson, had bought it back. The changes in the boardroom meant Phil and I had lost a valuable ally.

The results were not all disastrous. Wins against Bolton, Wigan, Stoke and Manchester City kept our head above water. However, the next three were lost and after the last defeat, a 5-1 mauling at Goodison Park, we were back in the relegation zone on goal difference. Phil thought the best way to recover from that was not to hammer the players but for the fitness coach to take them on a jog to the Humber Bridge and back.

During the defeat to Everton there had been a clash between Nicky Barmby and Jimmy Bullard, who had blamed Barmby for a goal we had conceded in the first half and the row had continued in the dressing room. Nicky was a top professional who could be spiky and was rightly proud of his levels of performance.

I did not mind players having a go at each other in the dressing room. Sometimes, you need to hear a different voice to the manager, someone you trained with, someone you played alongside. Alan Mullery used to tell us that, if Tottenham were struggling, Bill Nicholson would wait outside the dressing room while his captain, Dave Mackay, laid down the law. He would tear into his team-mates.

When I was at Brighton, Mullery would come into the dressing room and have a go and when he had left the players would start moaning about what he had said. That used to infuriate me. I told them they should have it out with the manager and tell Alan to his face what they thought. It was usually better that way.

However, by Monday the row was still going on and it flared up again at the bridge where Jimmy went for Nicky. There was a punch-up, Bullard had to be restrained and all of it was played out in front of a group from the local Women's Institute who were being given a guided tour of the Humber Bridge.

When we heard about it, we could not believe what had happened. Soon it was on the radio, on Sky Sports, in the press and it did us absolutely no favours at all. The club was forced to make a public apology.

We would be at home to Arsenal in the Saturday evening kick-off live on television. Early on, Andrei Arshavin skipped through our defence to put Arsenal ahead but Sol Campbell gave a penalty away which Bullard converted.

Once George Boateng had been sent off, Hull had to play with ten men for virtually the entire second half. We held out until the third minute of stoppage time when Boaz Myhill palmed a shot from Denilson straight into Nicklas Bendtner's path. Arsenal won, 2-1.

Boaz was distraught – it had been a straightforward enough save – but it would be very hard to criticise him. Boaz had been one of those who had been with Hull through all four divisions and he had saved us many, many times.

Because Arsène Wenger never used to come for a drink after a match, Phil and I didn't really know what to do with ourselves afterwards. We were in the office, very downcast, we didn't feel like having a drink and we went home. I told Phil I would see him on Monday morning.

On Mondays, I would leave my home in Cheadle at around six in the morning and would be at Hull at half seven or quarter to eight. On the way, I got a call from Phil Brown who said: 'I've been summoned to the ground by Adam Pearson, what do you think?'

'I'll tell you what I think, Phil. We have Portsmouth away on Saturday and I think that game will define our careers here.'

Portsmouth were enduring an awful time. They were in administration, bottom of the Premier League, and had difficulty paying their players. They would, however, reach the FA Cup Final. If we failed to beat them, we would be at serious risk of the sack.

Half an hour later, Phil rang back in tears. 'I've had the sack. Adam Pearson has just fired me.'

I could not understand it because, as we were milling around our office at the KC Stadium on Saturday night, Adam Pearson had come in and said: 'If we keep playing like we did against Arsenal, we will stay up.'

Pearson rang and said he needed to see me. He said he might want me and Steve Parkin to prepare the team for Saturday's game at Fratton Park. I would be taking training that morning.

When I was a manager, I would always say to my backroom staff: 'If I get the sack, I want the rest of you to sit tight. I don't want you doing anything stupid, like walking out in sympathy or refusing to work with the new manager. You all have mortgages to pay.'

Phil said the same thing. He called a meeting with the players to explain what had happened and some of them were in tears. The guys who had been through the divisions with Hull were particularly affected. Phil had looked after them financially and the bonus system we had in place was very good.

On Wednesday, which was our day off, Adam Pearson rang and said he had spoken to three or four managers who had turned him down but he had decided to appoint Iain Dowie.

I said: 'Do you not think Steve and I are good enough to take charge until the end of the season?'

'No. I think Iain Dowie is a better option. Come in tomorrow and I will sort your contract out.' Steve Parkin and Bob Shaw were kept on and my contract was paid up in full.

On the Friday, I said to Val: 'I cannot sit in this living room and watch the Jeff Stelling show and see all the results come in.' Normally, I love *Soccer Saturday* but this would have been too much.

We booked a hotel in the Lake District. I had a few drinks and tried to pay no attention to the football. When someone phoned with the latest score from Fratton Park, I told them I did not want to know. Hull were leading until two late goals saw Portsmouth win, 3-2.

Hull won their next game at home to Fulham but didn't win any of their last seven matches and went down. After Charlton and Newcastle, it was the third relegation Dowie had been involved with.

I like to think that had Phil stayed we would have had a better chance of survival. The fans were not calling for his dismissal, heads had not gone down in the dressing room. To be sacked after losing to Arsenal in the 93rd minute was a harsh decision. We deserved better.

Paul Duffen (chairman Hull City 2007–2009)

I was running a media business which had become a public company in 2000 and was becoming tired of teenaged fund managers telling me how to run it. I was asked if I would front a bid to buy West Ham United from Terry Brown. Very inconsiderately, West Ham got themselves promoted in 2005 which pushed the price up from £20m to £60m.

Our little consortium couldn't handle that and the next club I did due diligence on was Cardiff City. Sam Hammam was the owner but his son was more prominent at Ninian Park than he was and the chairman, Peter Ridsdale, had no equity or authority but had the builder who could redevelop the stadium. There was no co-ordination between the three of them and it became impossible to do a deal.

The next ball out of the hat was Hull City, which was perfect. It had a huge catchment area. The nearest significant club to the west is Leeds United, to the north is Middlesbrough and south is Leicester with nothing much in between.

There was a passionate fan base, a new stadium and 104 years of history. I went to live in Leeds and saw every game, home and away, with the cover story that I was an advisor to the board. I saw Phil Brown keep the club up and we finished 21st. I became chairman in June 2007.

I had been impressed with what Phil had done, I liked the way he was in tune with the players and the fans. I remember one game at Barnsley, where after we had been badly beaten, Phil stood by the tunnel and clapped them off. I met him in the Malmaison in Leeds and offered him a contract.

Brian was the key appointment. I met him first at a box in the West Stand at Hull in late June. I had gone to Lancing College in Sussex and I had seen Brian play for Brighton under Alan Mullery so I knew there was a feisty little bastard hidden beneath all the politeness.

I thought it was a brave appointment by Phil because, if it all went horribly wrong, Brian was a ready-made replacement. Brian had a strong affiliation with the supporters and, had Phil stumbled, it would have been very easy for me to make the switch. It proved a great combination because while Phil had all the enthusiasm none of this was new to Brian. He had done it all before. He gave the club a sense of maturity.

I think he has changed over time but when he took over at Hull, Phil was very collaborative and consultative. He wanted input from everyone. Brian would sit next to me in the directors' box, on a microphone link to Phil, and I became immersed in Brian's perspective of the game. When I first started going into the directors' box, I would sit next to two directors who just talked to each other throughout the game. To me, that was a nonsense. I wanted to learn.

Steve Parkin, who was the first-team coach, was a traditionalist who didn't like the idea of the chairman coming to the training ground or being involved in the rituals of match day. I could understand that because the insecurities of football coaching meant you wanted to keep what went on at the training ground away from the board. Gradually, Steve came to realise that we weren't trying to interfere, we wanted to learn and that we would never come uninvited.

Of course, we were not ready for the Premier League. We had gone up two years ahead of schedule but, given that Hull had never played top-flight football in its history, you can argue that it never would have been ready.

The pressures off the pitch that come from being promoted to the Premier League are as great as those on the pitch. At least on the pitch you know what is coming at you. Off the pitch it was like throwing a wedding every other week for 25,000 people. Every away game meant we had 3,000 tickets to sell and 10,000 who wanted to buy them.

The composition of your dressing room will change. A third will be foreign footballers, probably on our budget,

French-African footballers. It is the only way you can afford to build your squad. You will get some high-maintenance footballers who you think you can turn around and there were those who had been with the club as Hull were promoted through three divisions. Your dressing room became as eclectic as the bar in the *Star Wars* film.

You had to ask yourself if Ian Ashbee, the hero who captained Hull from the bottom to the top division, would make the team sheet in the Premier League. He did but there was no way Wayne Brown was going to play Premier League football and you ended up with his wife bawling me out in a Manchester nightclub telling me how disloyal I was.

I had three summer transfer windows with Phil and Brian and the first in 2007 was the most important. It was a complete overhaul of the squad and Brian's contacts were critical to getting Fraizer Campbell out of Manchester United.

Richard Garcia, whom we bought from Colchester, would not have passed any medical now. He had suffered some terrible injuries but would run through brick walls for the cause. The first signing was Dean Windass, who had been on loan from Bradford.

There were no prima donnas in that promotion season, just wholehearted footballers. There are similarities between that Hull team and the Sheffield United side that Chris Wilder took up to the Premier League, with the caveat that Sheffield United had a history of playing top-flight football which Hull lacked in 2008.

Walking down Wembley Way, I had no doubt we would win the play-off final. Momentum was with us and it was the first time Hull had ever played at Wembley. We had achieved something just by getting there.

I had no input on tactics or team selection – I was simply not qualified – but I was sometimes told how Hull would play. On the morning of our game against Arsenal at the Emirates Stadium, I was having breakfast with Phil Brown and he said: 'Nobby Horton and I have been going through our game plan against Arsenal and we're going to attack.

'If we try to shut up shop, we will probably lose 3-0. If we go for it, we might lose by seven but we might just win.' I thought that an excellent strategy, particularly early in the season when the adrenaline was still high. We won, 2-1. Hull still hold the Premier League record for the most points by a promoted side after ten games. We had 20 points after nine matches.

Then, things began to slide and we faced Manchester United on the last game of the season knowing we could be relegated. Hull would have coped with relegation. Just as we had gone up with no baggage, we would have gone down with no baggage. We didn't have 500 staff and practically all of our players had relegation clauses in their contracts.

I stepped down in 2009 and the reason was that we had run out of money. We were being bankrolled by an Essex property investor called Russell Bartlett, who wanted no acknowledgement of his role at Hull City. I was the front man and people assumed I owned the football club.

However, when Ken Bates got into difficulties over who actually owned Leeds United, the FA insisted on full disclosure of beneficial ownership. It coincided with a meltdown in the British property market. As someone who invested heavily in property, it left Russell exposed and he had to take cash out of the football club in order to meet his obligations. The club appointed an insolvency practitioner to sit on the board and I left.

Russell had had no part in the running of the club, he had simply turned up to Hull in his helicopter on match days and then went back to Essex. When we left, Adam Pearson was brought back into the club to be the new chairman because he was practically the only person Russell Bartlett knew in football.

He sacked Phil, cleaned out Brian and Steve, Hull were relegated and Adam himself was fired. Russell came back as chairman before everything melted down and the club was sold to the Allams for a pound.

It ended one of the most intense periods of my life. I was chairman for just over 100 games and I had more experiences in that time than some people who had been running a club for 1,000.

Here, There and Everywhere

(Games 1,817–2,118)

YOU might have thought that, having taken Hull from the brink of relegation to League One to the Premier League, Phil Brown and I might have had plenty of credit in the managerial bank. You might have thought we would have fixed ourselves up with a job pretty quickly.

With its limited number of jobs, that is not how football works and eight months after our dismissal we were still unemployed.

To keep ourselves busy, Phil and I would watch games so we would be in touch with what was happening and, sometimes, to meet up with people we knew.

Three days after Christmas, I suggested to Phil that we go to Deepdale to watch Preston play Middlesbrough. It was a decision that would wreck my friendship with Sir Alex Ferguson. His son, Darren, was manager of Preston. They were bottom of the Championship and facing

Middlesbrough, who were only out of the relegation zone on goal difference.

At first glance, this might seem like a really calculated move – two football men going to a game where both clubs are in trouble. This is something I have never done. I think it abhorrent for out-of-work managers to be visible at clubs where the manager is fighting for his life.

However, the facts were that Tony Mowbray had been appointed as Middlesbrough manager a couple of months before. Mowbray was a legend at Middlesbrough, who in 1986 had been made captain of a side that had gone into administration and faced closure. He captained them back to the top flight and as manager was steering them away from the drop. At the time, he was unsackable.

I thought the same of Darren Ferguson. Preston may have been bottom but they were owned by Trevor Hemmings, who had owned three Grand National winners and was one of the richest men in Britain. He was also good friends with Alex Ferguson. It seemed impossible to believe he would jeopardise that friendship by firing his son. The day after Middlesbrough had won 3-1 at Deepdale, Hemmings did just that.

A few days later, Phil, who owned racehorses with Sam Allardyce and other Bolton players, and I went to Haydock Park, where we bumped into Trevor Hemmings in the owners' and trainers' enclosure.

During the conversation Hemmings, who had approached other managers, asked why Phil had not applied for the Preston job. Phil said: 'Okay, I'll apply for it.' He got an interview and he got the job. I was appointed as his assistant.

The day after Darren's sacking, Alex Ferguson called Preston's chairman, Maurice Lindsay, and recalled his loan players to Manchester United. David Unsworth, who had taken over as caretaker, was forced to do without the striker, Joshua King, and the defender, Richie de Laet. Ferguson also told Maurice that he wanted Matty James, an England Under-20 midfielder who was on a longer-term deal, not to play for Preston again.

Immediately afterwards, Tony Pulis, who is very close to Ferguson, recalled two of his players – Michael Tonge and Danny Pugh – to Stoke. Pulis claimed they were needed back at the Britannia Stadium.

Pugh was given games but, as it turned out, Michael Tonge played only one match for Stoke in the rest of the season – coming on as a substitute in an FA Cup tie at Cardiff.

Maurice Lindsay likened what had happened to having 'all four tyres punctured on a car'.

All this happened before we were appointed. When the announcement was made that Phil Brown and I had replaced Darren, Fergie was apparently furious with us and we have barely spoken since.

A hole had been ripped in the squad and we knew survival would be difficult. We began with an FA Cup tie against Nottingham Forest, which was lost, 2-1.

In the league there were far too many draws and we did not win a match until 15 March, more than three months after we had taken over. Preston were still bottom of the table but they were now 15 points from safety.

Three straight wins over Scunthorpe, Leicester and Swansea, who were managed by Brendan Rodgers, were only enough to take us up one place in the division. We were relegated after a 1-0 defeat by Cardiff with two matches of the season still to go.

We had to rebuild and make cutbacks and earned £750,000 by selling Keith Tracy, a midfielder who was an Ireland international, to Burnley.

Had the club sanctioned a seventh of that fee to buy Jamie Vardy, our story at Preston might have had a very different outcome. Vardy was playing for Halifax, as a winger rather than a striker. My old number two, Dennis Booth, who was very good at spotting this type of potential, had tried to sign him for Carlisle when Vardy was playing for Stocksbridge.

I had watched Vardy and, as Phil had once played for Halifax, he was aware of him. Halifax quoted us a fee of £100,000, which Preston thought was too much. Fleetwood, who were then in the Conference, paid the money and in 2012, after winning promotion to the Football League, they sold Vardy to Leicester for £1m.

We prepared for the season at a training camp run by the Royal Marines at Arbroath. The boys slept on sleeping bags in two large halls. They trained on the sand dunes and, if anyone was late, it was straight into the North Sea. There were assault courses and night exercises where they were taken out and subjected to sleep deprivation.

We were told they would kidnap one of our players and the rest of the squad would have to find them. Phil joined in but I was in a tent on a camp bed when I heard a rustling outside and then there was a marine trying to get in before he saw me and said: 'Sorry, didn't realise it was you.'

Our League One season began with a 4-2 defeat at home to Colchester followed by a 1-1 draw with Scunthorpe who had been relegated with us.

The poor start was deceptive. We played a diamond formation with Neil Mellor spearheading the attack. Neil had played for Liverpool, where he will always be remembered for a fabulous goal against Arsenal. I had played with his father, Ian, at Brighton.

Neil scored our first goal of the season and scored twice in games against Yeovil, Brentford and Wycombe. However, he had been dogged by injuries at Liverpool and his luck did not get any better at Preston.

Jamie Proctor was another of the stand-out performers in the early part of the season. He was a teenager, a local lad and a real athlete, who had scored in Preston's last game of the season – a victory over Watford when we had already been relegated.

He forced his way in through some of the best pre-season performances I have ever seen. He scored ten goals in seven games, including a hat-trick against Fleetwood. However, at the end of October, he had to undergo a hernia operation. Preston's other striker, Iain Hume, who carried an 18-inch scar after being elbowed in the head while playing for Barnsley, was also injured after scoring six goals in the first three months of the season.

With them in the side, Preston had been in superb form. After the draw at Scunthorpe, we won eight of the next nine. Preston were second in the table, two points behind Charlton but with a game in hand.

Without our front three, we fell away badly. We were forced to field some very young players. At 16, Brendon Zibaka was until recently the youngest footballer to play for Preston. He was joined by Doyle Middleton, a 5ft 3in midfielder, Scott Leather and Shannon Clucas. They were good, willing lads but to fill in for seasoned first-team footballers was too much for them.

Preston won one of their next 11 matches and after a goalless draw against Stevenage in December left us tenth, Phil and I were fired. It was the first time in nearly 30 years as a manager that I had been sacked over the phone.

Shortly beforehand, Maurice Lindsay, the Preston chairman, who was perhaps better known for his work in rugby league with Wigan Warriors, had suffered a knee injury, which had then turned septic and forced his resignation.

His replacement was Peter Ridsdale, who as chairman of Leeds had overseen the club's dramatic rise and fall. He had called a meeting with Phil Brown at White's, the hotel built into the Reebok Stadium in Bolton.

Ridsdale said: 'I have terminated Phil's contract and I am terminating yours.'

'What, over the phone?'

'You can come over to Bolton and see me.'

'What's the point? I think I deserve more respect than that.'

I had actually met Peter Ridsdale the day before. Preston were playing Stoke in the FA Youth Cup and I had talked to him during the game and did not think anything more of it. If he wanted to get rid of me, then would have been a good time to do it.

I enjoyed my time at Preston. It is a club with tradition and history full of good people like Jim McCluskey, who was the club's chief scout and Dean Ramsdale, who was director of youth and who now works for Manchester City.

A few months later in March came the decision to return to Macclesfield to try to keep them from falling out of the Football League. It was a decision I regretted almost the moment I made it.

In March 2013, Phil Brown was offered the job of managing Southend United, whose bid to make the League Two play-offs had been tailing off. We met the chairman, Ron Martin, at Manchester Airport and Phil offered me the opportunity to come to Essex with him but, frankly, it seemed too far away. Southend finished in 11th place in League Two.

In his first full season at Roots Hall, Phil took Southend to the play-offs only to see them lose in the semi-finals to Burton. By then, I had accepted an offer from Paul Dickov to become his assistant at Doncaster.

Despite our common Manchester City connection, I didn't know Paul that well – Alan Ball had signed him from Arsenal just before he was sacked in 1996. I took a phone call saying Paul was looking for an assistant but I heard nothing more and went on a cruise still checking my phone for any updates.

Eventually, I was offered a contract. Doncaster had just been promoted to the Championship, going up with Bournemouth and Yeovil. Brian Flynn, who had taken them up, had asked to concentrate on developing young players and was made director of football.

Paul Dickov, whose time at Oldham had been notable for knocking Liverpool out of the FA Cup, was brought in to replace Brian and I was to perform much the same role with him that I had with Phil Brown.

We were not as close as Phil and I had been and the relationship was rather more distant. Paul was a younger man who had his own ideas and I respected that. I had been working with Phil for four years and sometimes it is hard to make the adjustment to someone else's way of working.

Most of his team were men around Paul's age. Paul Butler was a young, inexperienced coach who would go on to become assistant manager at Leeds. Paul Gerrard, who had replaced Neville Southall at Everton, excelled as a goalkeeping coach as did Ben Rome as fitness coach.

John Ryan was the owner. He had run a plastic surgery business and overseen the move from the ramshackle Belle Vue to the Keepmoat Stadium. His money had taken them from the Conference to the Championship.

Doncaster used Gerry Taggart as a part-time chief scout so I would fill in, watching many more games than I had done at Hull. They had two wonderful women in the kitchens called Samantha and Vicki who would make me up some sandwiches if I had to go to a night game.

The problem Doncaster suffered from was inconsistency. We began well, beating Blackburn at home and drawing at Wigan, who were the FA Cup holders, but it was not until March that we had back-to-back wins in the league.

Then, we beat Huddersfield and Watford at the Keepmoat, with Billy Sharp scoring in both games. Billy, whom we had taken on loan from Southampton, was an amazing man, another of those who played in all four divisions. At the end of March, at Leeds, he finished off a move that involved 28 passes.

Doncaster played astonishingly well at Elland Road and the win left us 18th, four places and eight points above the drop zone. We seemed safe. There were seven matches left. We took one point from them – a goalless draw at Millwall.

Nevertheless, on the last day of the season, Doncaster still had their fate in their own hands. We were one place and one point above the relegation zone. Barnsley and Yeovil had already been relegated and we would join them if Birmingham bettered our result. We would be away to Leicester; Birmingham would be at Bolton.

Leicester had 99 points and they would parade the Championship trophy at the King Power Stadium. They had lost one league game since November. Bolton had nothing to play for.

Our keeper, Sam Johnstone, whom we had brought in on loan from Manchester United, made a string of fine saves. With a quarter of an hour to go, we seemed on course to survive. We were holding Leicester and Birmingham were two down at the Reebok Stadium.

Then, we gave away a soft penalty which David Nugent scored. Leicester won the match, 1-0, in bright sunshine and we had to wait for the news from Bolton. There, Birmingham had scored twice in the final 12 minutes to force a draw and relegate Doncaster on goal difference.

In terms of ability, Doncaster would be in the bottom half of the Championship or the top half of League One. We had enough to survive and to go down like that felt ridiculous, especially after that win at Leeds. Going back from Elland Road everyone, players and staff, felt we were safe and perhaps that is what killed us. I felt we should have done something like changing the system to stop the rot. One point would have done it.

The summer was spent reducing the wage bill. Eleven players left the Keepmoat, only one of whom – James Husband, who went to Middlesbrough – attracted a fee. We signed eight players without paying a fee and brought in another six on loan. The pre-season which began at Bradford Park Avenue was my 50th in football.

The season that followed was a disappointment. Again, we were inconsistent. Doncaster did not manage back-to-back wins until just before Christmas, although by February we had made the play-off places. However, the season tailed off and Doncaster finished 13th.

Gerry Taggart was promoted to become Paul Dickov's number two and I was let go. I wasn't, however, let go for very long because Phil Brown offered me a second chance to go to Southend.

It was a different offer because in 2013 I had been asked to go as Phil's number two. That would have meant working full time and probably moving house, which at 64 I wasn't prepared to do. This time I was to be 'football co-ordinator', which was director of football by another name. I would watch games in the north on Southend's behalf and come down on Thursdays to prepare for the weekend matches. As he had done at Hull, Bob Shaw would be working alongside me as chief scout. As I had done at Hull, Phil wanted me to bounce ideas off him.

Part of my job was to examine different parts of the club, which was run from a rather ramshackle training ground called Boots and Laces, which at one time had been a nightclub.

It was used by the first team and the kids and I was impressed by the academy manager, Ricky Duncan, who had overhauled the youth system at Southend – which is something the club is now reaping the benefits of.

Ricky had put together a good team – Kevin Maher, who had played nearly 400 league games for Southend, looked after the under-21s. Ian Hart and Dave Huzzey ran the coaching and Lis Orford administered the centre. In youth-team football at least Southend United punched above its weight.

Phil had just taken Southend up to League One via the play-offs. The final, against Wycombe, was nothing if not dramatic. Joe Piggott scored for Southend in stoppage time of extra time to force a penalty shoot-out which Southend won 7-6.

I would stay in a beautiful hotel at Thorpe Bay, called the Roslin, while Phil had an apartment on the seafront. Sometimes my wife and daughter, Lucy, would come down on the Friday.

For a promoted club, Southend did pretty well. By February, we were outside the play-off places on goal difference. However, we lost our last five games to finish 14th. Doncaster, with Darren Ferguson in charge, were relegated to League Two.

Looking back, we had built a platform for a season that might have seen Southend promoted to the Championship. There is one match in that 2016/17 season that sticks in my throat.

It came in February. We had just beaten Scunthorpe, who were fighting it out with Sheffield United at the top of League One, to take us into the play-off positions.

Southend's next game was at Millwall and was refereed by Andre Marriner, who would usually be in charge of Premier League fixtures and had just been announced as the referee for the League Cup Final between Manchester United and Southampton.

In the first half Marriner sent off our midfielder, Will Atkinson, for a tackle on Tony Craig that was at most a yellow card. Then, in the last minute, Craig brought down Jermaine McGlashan for what was one of the more blatant penalties I have seen in my career. Andre Marriner waved it away. I usually did the referees' reports for Southend and I contacted David Allison, the referees' assessor, who told me that, on the feedback he had received, it was a penalty.

It might seem strange to dwell on a single penalty call in a 46-game season. We might have missed the penalty but, had we scored from it, Southend would have finished sixth, one place ahead of Millwall. In the play-off final, Millwall beat Bradford to reach the Championship. We had taken four points off Bradford in the league. We would have fancied our chances.

That is how football people think when they sift through a season. If you've finished mid-table or been relegated in last place, there is no point dwelling on it. However, if you miss out by a point, as Southend did, then you look for a game which should have made a difference and for Phil and me Millwall away was it.

The following month, we had a match on a Tuesday night at Coventry. The plan had been for the players to go to the

Cheltenham Festival the next day. However, we had played so badly on the Saturday at Bristol Rovers that Phil had cancelled the event and the players didn't take their suits for the festival.

Southend beat Coventry, 2-0, at the Ricoh Arena and the players kept hassling Phil to let them go to Cheltenham. He pointed out that they had nothing to wear. Fortunately, there was a big Tesco near the hotel and they all trooped over and bought shoes, ties and suits. They won the next match, 3-2, at home to Walsall, and the two after that.

Nile Ranger scored in all four of those matches. He had the ability to be anything he wanted. He was from north London but had made his name at Newcastle. Nile had had disciplinary problems at every club he had signed for which by the time he reached Roots Hall, included Barnsley, Swindon and Blackpool.

He had been convicted for online banking fraud and served ten weeks in prison which meant he had to wear an electronic tag and was subjected to a curfew. Until the curfew was lifted, he could not play in an evening kick-off. When he was finally allowed to play, he scored against Fleetwood.

I spoke to him a lot. I could not quite get my head round why he could not see how far he could go in the game with his ability. All he had to do was to conform a little and that was something he could not do.

He was a big, strong, powerful footballer. Sheffield United would be promoted to the Championship that season on their way to the Premier League under Chris

Wilder. We faced them at Bramall Lane in August and Nile Ranger was unplayable. Southend were three up after a quarter of an hour but in the 24th minute of the match, Nile went up for a challenge and turned his ankle over and had to be taken off.

The following season, Nile scored only twice which may have been one of the reasons why it was our last at Roots Hall. We beat Blackburn in our opening fixture but we didn't win again until the end of September when we beat Fleetwood who were managed by Uwe Rösler. We were never more than mid-table.

The end came in January 2018, just after we had sold Ryan Leonard, a good defensive midfielder, to Sheffield United for £711,000. We lost 2-1 to Fleetwood at Roots Hall and that was that. Uwe Rösler, the man I had brought into English football, got me the sack.

We knew we were not doing brilliantly but given that Ron Martin had called a meeting to discuss player recruitment that would be funded by the Leonard transfer only days before, we assumed Southend would give us more time.

Once more I was sacked by phone. I was at Mottram Hall on a day off when a Southend number appeared on my phone and Ron Martin told me Phil Brown and Bob Shaw had been sacked. My contract, too, was being terminated.

I felt for Phil. He had spent nearly five years at Southend and had managed them from League Two to League One and might have promoted them to the Championship, which surely was the very limit of where football might take Southend United.

Ron Martin had been a member of Britain's bobsleigh team in the 1980 Winter Olympics at Lake Placid but he was pretty slow when it came to paying us the balance of our contracts. We had to get the League Managers' Association involved. Management is a stressful, precarious existence at the best of times. The one thing managers ought to be able to count on when they are thrown on to the dole is that they will be paid.

Two months later, Phil was appointed as manager of Swindon and offered me my last job in football as his assistant. Swindon were ninth in League Two but they were only out of the play-off positions on goal difference. Our job was getting them into the play-offs.

We had ten games. We won the first at Cambridge and the last at home to Accrington, who went up as champions, and none in between. Some of the performances in between were really poor. Swindon finished the season where we had found them – in ninth.

Swindon 3, Accrington Stanley 0 was the final game of football I was to be involved with professionally. It was nearly 48 years since my first, when I came up against Archie Gemmill in Port Vale's 1-0 win over Preston in September 1970.

You always know it's your debut, you are never quite sure when you leave the ground that this will be your last match.

I thought that, with the players we had available, Swindon should at least have got into the play-offs. To have finished ninth was a real failure and I told Phil that.

I also said that I wasn't prepared to carry on as his number two. It would have been unfair to him because my heart was not in commuting backwards and forwards from Cheshire to Wiltshire to help run the club on a full-time basis. Phil said he understood.

A few days later, Val and I flew off to Dubai for a holiday and to get away from a lifetime in football.

A Life in Football

IT says something for how long I have been involved in the game that many of the grounds on which I played and managed no longer exist.

Boothferry Park has gone. The Manor Ground in Oxford is now a hospital, Maine Road has been turned into a housing estate. Kenilworth Road will soon disappear. The one I miss most is the Goldstone Ground. When it was full there was no sound like it.

When I went there in 1976, people told me that Brighton was not a football town. They only had to go to the Goldstone and hear the crowd to know how wrong that statement was.

We saw Brighton's passion for football in our wage packets because we were on a crowd bonus scheme. If the crowd was between 10–15,000, we would be paid £10 per thousand. If it was more than 15,000, we would be on £15 per thousand.

In our promotion seasons, we thought we had won the Pools because we would be on win and crowd bonuses that would be paid out regularly. When I went back to manage

Brighton in 1998, I missed the Goldstone Ground terribly. I felt I was at a club that had had its heart ripped out.

As a player, Brighton was probably where I was happiest. It was the first time I had known real success as a footballer and by making me captain Peter Taylor and Alan Mullery put me at the centre of a side that was to be promoted through two divisions.

There are obvious differences in how young footballers are treated then and now. When I was an apprentice at Walsall, we would sweep the terraces at Fellows Park – which is now a Morrisons supermarket. We would clean the boots of the first-team players, we would scrub the baths after matches, pick the kit off the dressing-room floor. The fact that as a player at Port Vale I only trained twice a week with the team seems ludicrous now.

When you did train, even when you were training with a top-flight club as I did with Brighton and Luton, there was not much talk of tactics or showing you films of how your opponents might play.

When Alan Mullery gave his team talks at Brighton, his focus would be almost entirely on the way we played. Brian Clough, famously, never mentioned the opposition when he addressed his players at Derby and Nottingham Forest.

Now players at every level would be shown DVDs of the opposition that would focus on how they attack, how they defend, what tricks certain players use, how they signal their routines from a set piece.

It was only when I went to Luton in 1981 and met David Pleat that things became more recognisable to a modern footballer. On the pitch on a Friday, David would make us do shadow-play which was 11 against nobody, where you went through the routines the manager would want to see on match day and where you got a sense of where you should be when the ball was passed. I was 32 before I ever did shadow-play. I thought it was revolutionary and it became part of the techniques I used when I was a manager.

Fridays at Luton would be far more relaxed than at Port Vale or Brighton. There would be shadow-play, we would practise taking and defending free kicks or throw-ins but not much more.

I still keep in touch with the game and work with Laura Woolf at Road3 as a judge at the Northwest Football Awards which are staged at the Old Trafford cricket ground. Despite the fact that her partner, Daniel, is a big Manchester United fan we have become good friends.

I go to the Etihad Stadium a lot. Manchester City look after me and my family wonderfully. I speak at meetings of the club's supporters' association branches. Even after all the success they have had at the Etihad, Manchester City fans still have a deep interest in what happened at Maine Road.

Every time I go to a branch meeting, three fanatical Manchester City fans accompany me – George Gibbons, Steve Jenkins and Paul Farmer, who is our driver. He is happy to have a cup of tea while we have a few beers.

Watching the fabulous Manchester City side that Pep Guardiola has created, it seems pointless to deny that the game has got quicker, better and more entertaining. Throughout my career, I have never stopped learning, never stopped being intrigued by new ideas and watching Manchester City train now would be an education.

At Vincent Kompany's testimonial dinner, it was announced that I had just turned 70, which prompted Pep Guardiola to come over to our table. I spoke to him like a schoolboy, overcome with nerves.

I don't have regrets. I am proud of the fact that my career took me from non-league football with Hednesford to what would now be the Premier League with Brighton and Luton.

In those 14 years I had only five managers – Gordon Lee, Roy Sproson, Peter Taylor, Alan Mullery and David Pleat. I owe them all something. Gordon Lee took me from non-league football. Peter Taylor began my career at Brighton.

Alan Mullery was instrumental in giving me the mindset to become a manager. He would say to me: 'If you see anything that needs changing on the pitch, I want you to do it, without reference to me and I will back you.' David Pleat changed the way I looked at football.

I have played alongside some great footballers. From the moment Mark Lawrenson came to Brighton as a 20-year-old, you could tell he would become a great player. Ricky Hill at Luton possessed a skill and a work rate I have seldom come across. He should have played more than three times for England. David Moss, who was a fabulous winger at Kenilworth Road, should have had an international career. Paul Walsh had a top-flight career that lasted 13 years.

There was no better team I played against than the Liverpool side that dominated English football in the 1980s. In 1983, Luton had gone to Anfield and been thrashed 6-0. When we came into the dressing room, David Pleat came in and said: 'Well done.' I was thinking: 'Well done? We've lost by six. Is he taking the piss?'

It was the season Liverpool would win the Treble of the European Cup, the championship and the League Cup and David recognised that no team could live with them in that mood and that Luton had actually played some good football. There was no reason to rant or rave.

Individually, I can close my eyes and see some amazing opponents; Liam Brady, Glenn Hoddle, Graeme Souness. Then there was the man who was probably the most complete footballer I ever faced – Bryan Robson.

You knew, if you were marking Robson, that he would get in the box at least 12 times during a game. You knew, if he was running at you, that he would probably go past you. He was brave, he was strong, he was quick.

I remember the first time I faced him, when Bryan was playing for West Brom in 1979. He was 22 then and you could tell he was a good player. Ron Atkinson then took him to Manchester United, where he became a great footballer.

As a manager and a player, my career seldom stayed at one level. As a footballer I started out in the non-league game at Hednesford and finished in what would now be the Premier League at Luton. As a manager or an assistant, I experienced the Premier League with Manchester City and Hull and the very bottom of the league at Macclesfield.

I relished the time I spent managing Macclesfield and Port Vale. The pressures and the challenges are the same as they are in the Premier League – you have to win games of football with the players you have.

I always remembered where I came from. As a player and as a manager, I tried not to become carried away by the big time and when I was in the lower leagues, I never thought: 'I am too good for this.'

I always wanted to win and my wife and kids will tell you I was a different animal between three and five o'clock on a Saturday afternoon. Perhaps that's why, as a manager, I signed players like Andy Morrison, who also loathed losing.

I am proud of the fact that I was managing them when Macclesfield had the biggest home and away victories in their history. I had my 1,000th game as a manager at Macclesfield. I always wanted the best for whoever I was working for, whether it was Man City or Macc Town.

Every football club where I have played or managed has meant something. I have never left a club and hoped they got relegated or were humiliated because that would involve humiliating the good people you left behind. And there were so many good people.

If I were to meet my younger self, just starting out at Port Vale, or a young footballer now, I would tell them to enjoy the game. It is a great game and always has been. The thing is, even when you've done 50 years in football, it all goes by so very quickly.

Val Horton

When I met Brian I found my life changed utterly. What does set me apart from a lot of wives and girlfriends I have met, is that I do like football. So many managers' wives I know don't go to games.

When I was at the ground watching Brian's teams, I had to tell myself to behave. I knew I couldn't shout or scream so I tended to have this strangulated squeal. The final five minutes seem the longest of your life, your stomach is churning and you look at your watch every few seconds to try to speed it along. It gets to you. I was probably more stressed than he was.

My team was Manchester City and we went down to Wembley in 1999, where Brian was commentating on the play-off final against Gillingham. We had stopped at Warwick Services and as we went to leave, the Manchester City fans who were packed into the services began singing: 'There's only one Brian Horton.' It sends shivers down my spine thinking about it even now.

Before the game I was invited up to the gantry to sit alongside Brian while he was doing the commentary. It was so exciting for me and minutes from the end I could see the City fans streaming away thinking they had lost.

At away games, I tended to find myself at the end of the row of seats in the directors' box, pretty close to the home fans. In Hull's play-off semi-final at Watford, we won the first leg, 2-0, and one of the Watford fans next to me turned and said: 'It's not over yet.' I shouted at him: 'I think it is,' and then I realised I would have to leave pretty quickly.

Brian has a circle of friends in management but I don't have that with the managers' wives. I think we see each other as opponents and some may think that, if they are friendly to you, they might be letting their husbands down. Some simply avoid talking to you. I had a great relationship with Karen, who was Phil Brown's wife, and Kate Parkin who is married to Steve — but then we were on the same side.

I found I was treated quite well, probably better than most managers' wives. I don't think many are invited into the boardroom. I always was. At Macclesfield, I got friendly with the girl behind the bar in the boardroom and, if she was busy, I would help out serving drinks.

Brian and I were married on 5 October 2003. Getting married during a football season would not allow for a long honeymoon but the club gave us a couple of days off to go to Stratford-upon-Avon.

I have shared in some fantastic highs, such as seeing Hull promoted and going to Beijing with Hull for the Premier League Asia Trophy.

On the other hand, you have the awful days when Brian has had the sack and you are hurting for your husband. It hurts you as much as it hurts him because you are thinking: 'How dare they do that to him.'

At home, you learn to be on your own, he could be out two or three nights a week going to games. In the early days, I would go with him to watch a player. Later on, I would leave him to it but I would never say: 'Do you have to go?' It was his career; it was his life. Of course, he had to go.

Matthew Horton

Dad was managing Manchester City when I first really became aware of what he did for a living. After a home game when the stands had cleared and everyone was packing up, I would grab a ball from dad's office, take it on to the pitch and kick it around with the empty stands above me. It was a wonderful feeling. It was a unique experience, especially for a football-obsessed little boy.

When Huddersfield opened the McAlpine Stadium with a game against Blackburn, who were league champions, I was one of the mascots. Dad took me along to train with Huddersfield and Port Vale.

It was a different childhood because everybody at school knew what your family was up to and how well or badly your father was doing in his job.

When dad was relieved of his duties at Manchester City, there were photographers around the house in Wilmslow asking him to pose for a picture taking us to school – which he refused to do. Towards the end at Huddersfield you became aware of some pretty unkind comments from the fans but that was the exception. The experiences of being a football manager's son were nearly all positive.

What it does mean is that it dilutes the football team you support. I don't really have a club – although because of where we live I feel closest to Manchester City. You support whoever dad was involved with at the time. I didn't need to buy a paper or check the scores to know if dad's team had won or lost. You could tell the moment he walked through the door.

I went to King's School in Macclesfield, which was a strange choice for a football manager to send his son to because in the senior school they didn't play football. The sports on offer were cricket, which I loved and rugby, which I didn't.

You quickly learn that football is a kind of brotherhood. The people that dad has been involved with have all tended to have similar experiences – good and bad. They've had great days and they've probably had the sack and it binds them together.

You would meet them casually. One of my most vivid memories is of going into Blockbuster in Wilmslow and talking to David Beckham. Steve McClaren, whom dad knew from his days at Hull and Oxford, had arranged for me to get a signed Beckham shirt and I went in to thank him. We talked for about 20 minutes. What I had learned from dad was that, away from the pitch, footballers are normal people.

The toughest times were when dad was out of work – he would phone you two or three times a day. I never tried to persuade him to retire or tell him he has done his bit because football was his life. He could not live without football being a part of it.

Lucy Horton

I can still picture his old office at the Manor Ground in Oxford. I couldn't have been more than five when I went there but I remember it as being really dark and full of cigar smoke. After a game, we would go with the children of the club physio who were about the same age, and mess around in the gym.

I remember when we left Woodstock to move up to Manchester because Dad and I were in one car, totally not bothered by the move, while Mum and my brother were in the other car, crying their eyes out.

It was when he was managing Manchester City that you realised your dad might be famous. He would come and watch me play hockey and netball and one day I was doing a cross-country event. When it was over, I went looking for him and he was surrounded by all these kids. I was thinking: 'Dad, come and congratulate me.'

I can also remember City losing the Manchester derby, 5-0, to United and Matt becoming very upset and the guy who played Curly Watts on Coronation Street (Kevin

Kennedy) turning to him and saying: 'Don't worry, your dad will sort it out.'

Football was big in the 1990s but you only realised how massive it became when he was promoted with Hull City in 2008. That is when it hit you that he was in that bubble.

When he was at Macclesfield, I worked in the restaurant which overlooks the pitch and I could hear him, shouting and swearing at the players. The results wouldn't bother me but when he was with Hull in the Premier League, they did. The last three minutes of the play-off final at Wembley made me feel physically sick. When the final whistle went, Matt and I were almost crying.

I could always cope if I heard anything negative about Dad and in return you would get a lot of kudos growing up because you could tell people you met Robbie Williams or Victoria Beckham and when I was at Mottram Hall, I had my photo taken with David Beckham when I was ten.

I did work experience with the BBC when they were at Oxford Road in Manchester and I was taken to a Manchester City press conference by their City reporter, Ian Cheeseman. As we were leaving, Ian turned to the gateman at the training ground, who must have been with the club for 40 years and said: 'This is Brian Horton's daughter.'

He replied: 'Your dad was just the nicest man.'

That made me so proud because my father always said that no matter what you do or where you go be as nice as you can to everyone – because you will never know when you will meet them again and under what circumstances.

Also available at all good book stores

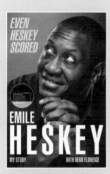

9781785315008

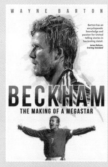

9781785316760

9781785314902

9781785314995

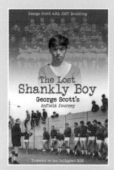

9781785316784

9781785316524

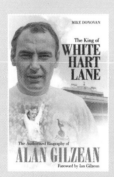

9781785315510

9781785316333

9781785316500